The Life
and
Selected Works
of
Rupert Brooke

The Life and Selected Works of Rupert Brooke

by

John Frayn Turner

Pen & Sword
MILITARY

First published in Great Britain in 1992 by
Breese Books (A division of Martin Breese International)

This revised and updated edition published in 2004 by
Pen & Sword Military
an imprint of
Pen & Sword Books Ltd
47 Church Street
Barnsley
South Yorkshire
S70 2AS

ISBN 1 84415 139 5

A CIP catalogue record for this book is
available from the British Library

Typeset in 11/13 Sabon by
Phoenix Typesetting, Auldgirth, Dumfriesshire

Printed and bound in England by
CPI UK

Pen & Sword Books Ltd incorporates the imprints of Pen & Sword
Aviation, Pen & Sword Maritime, Pen & Sword Military, Wharncliffe
Local History, Pen & Sword Select, Pen & Sword Military Classics and
Leo Cooper.

For a complete list of Pen & Sword titles please contact
PEN & SWORD BOOKS LIMITED
47 Church Street, Barnsley, South Yorkshire, S70 2AS, England
E-mail: enquiries@pen-and-sword.co.uk
Website: www.pen-and-sword.co.uk

Contents

Alphabetical List
of Selected Poems

Acknowledgements

The following gave me their personal help during my research for this book and I shall always feel deeply indebted to them: Bertrand Russell, St. John Ervine, Hugh Dalton, Basil Dean, Mrs Lascelles Abercrombie, Mrs Helen Bailey, John Schroder, Headmaster of Rugby School, Librarian of King's College Library, Cambridge University. My thanks also go to Martin Breese.

I am also grateful to be allowed to refer to these books:

Collected Poems of Rupert Brooke (Sidgwick and Jackson)
Letters from America by Rupert Brooke (Sidgwick and Jackson)
Call Back Yesterday by Hugh Dalton (Frederick Muller)
Between Two Worlds by John Middleton Murry (Jonathan Cape)
At Antwerp and the Dardanelles by Henry Foster (Mills and Boon)
The Golden Echo by David Garnett (Chatto and Windus)
Looking Back by Norman Douglas (Chatto and Windus)
For Remembrance by A. St. John Adcock (Hodder and Stoughton)
Recollections of Rupert Brooke by Maurice Browne (Alexander Greene)

I have also read the following books with considerable interest:

Rupert Brooke: His Life and His Legend by John Lehmann, *The Poems of Rupert Brooke* by Timothy Rogers, *A Little Love and Good Company* by Cathleen Nesbitt.

Introduction

It is especially apposite that Pen and Sword should be the publishers of this new edition of Rupert Brooke – because he lived for the pen and poetry, and died, if indirectly, serving the sword.

As well as retracing his life, the book now embraces a selection of all his major poems. By combining these two elements in a single volume, I have tried to convey the many facets of this remarkable man: the real Rupert Brooke, rather than the legend. I have aimed to reassess his poems. I hope that what emerges is, to some extent at least, an emotional essence of 'the splendour and the pain' in a brilliant if brief lifespan.

As the acknowledgements confirm, over the years I was fortunate enough to meet some of the illustrious luminaries who were Brooke's contemporaries. Also taking their place in any life of Rupert Brooke are the glittering literati from an unrepeatable era.

Brooke's living force of poetry – imperishable, inspired – has remained in print, almost obstinately, for some ninety years now. By offering his life and poems jointly, perhaps this book will help in some small measure to perpetuate Rupert Brooke's reputation as a poet of peace as well as of war. The pen and the sword . . .

John Frayn Turner
Leatherhead
August 2004

Part One

The Life
of
Rupert Brooke

Chapter One

The Rugby Years

Rupert Brooke was born on 3 August 1887, the year of Queen Victoria's Golden Jubilee. From his adolescence, though, he was vehemently anti-Victorian and detested the brand of imperialism bred by the nineteenth century. In fact, his whole being belonged to the twentieth century.

Brooke's birthplace was 5 Hillmorton Road, within sight of Rugby School, where his father had started teaching several years earlier. Their home stood only one road away from the School House, which Rupert came to know so well later on.

His father, William Parker Brooke, wore a walrus moustache and a spotted bow tie under the wing collar of the period. Being the son of a canon, Mr Brooke's vision remained cleanly conventional, although he was known to compose jocund verses in his rare lighter moments. Rupert's mother, Mary Ruth Cotterill, possessed a certain amount of money, over which she exercised the control of a straight and stern mind.

Into this formal family of the respectable late-Victorian middle class Rupert came to consciousness. But Hillmorton Road never imprinted more than an early memory, for in 1892, when Rupert was five, Mr Brooke received promotion to housemaster of School Field in Barby Road. With it went the house, so the family moved the few hundred yards and settled into their new home. Rupert's elder brother, Dick, was eleven by then, and Mrs Brooke had produced a third son, Alfred, when Rupert was three.

Almost as soon as they were installed at School Field, Rupert Brooke revealed his inherent unconventionality by wandering right away from the immediate world of the school and exploring every-thing in walking range. Once he was retrieved down by the Avon, another time roaming in the fields surrounding Rugby with his old bull terrier, mysteriously named Mister Pudsey Dawson.

But the full force of School Field with the environment of Rugby and its sprawling acres did not really reach him yet, for he was sent away to Hillbrow preparatory school. Just before he joined, Mrs Brooke led him into Rugby town to be photographed in his large, stiff Eton collar protruding over a velvet jacket. Completing the boy's correct attire were knickerbockers and long stockings. Rupert, aged seven, stood with his hands on his hips, his hair combed straight towards the front without a parting. He did not like that garb; in particular, he hated his Eton collar with its stiff, restricting feel. But as yet he was too young to rebel openly against such senseless conventions.

By 1898, he had graduated to a dark coat and waistcoat, with lighter trousers. He wore a large tie over the inevitable larger-still collar. Each year he resented those collars more. Now, at eleven, his proud, perfect features were well formed, and his lips might sometimes be parted with the upper one sloping slightly towards the centre.

Sir Gilbert Scott, the architect of School Field, recalls him at this time as delightful and intelligent. To these rare qualities for a boy could be added independence, for in 1899 he supported a local meeting in favour of the Boers! His mother told him off for trying to bully his younger brother into similar support, but Rupert countered with agility that it was she who was bullying for attempting to inflict her views on him.

Rupert was becoming an acute observer of life, with an enquiring intellect. Already he had developed a love of freedom and the unconventional, which could be ascribed at least in part to a revolt against the respectability of his background. He could not be bothered with the religious pieties of the family, and now his hate of formal clothes exploded into a fetish for an open neck wherever possible, and running about barefooted in summer. Rupert had a mind of his own: sensitive, strong.

Trim took the place of Mister Pudsey Dawson, the century closed and Rupert moved on from Hillbrow to Rugby itself; back home to his father's house and under the parental eyes. But his natural and growing enthusiasm and élan overcame any real resentment of the restrictions of Rugby. And all the while he gradually grew more conscious of his surroundings, his attitude towards them, his feelings for them; aware, if not yet articulate or able to express them clearly.

What was this school life, which would leave so indelible an impression on him? Rugby ranks as one of the first public schools, and was founded in 1567 by a man named Sheriff, who made his money in grocery. So it had existed since Elizabethan days, whose poets always attracted Rupert above all other periods. Many of the present buildings were far younger than this, though, the old cloistered quadrangle and the headmaster's house then being barely a century old. The new Big School was built as lately as 1885, while an expensive quadrangle celebrating the tercentenary of the foundation was finished soon after the Brookes moved into School Field.

Rupert looked up at the tall three-storey house as he returned to it in July 1901 for the summer holidays. This would be home over the next five years, home and school interwoven through his adolescence. School Field, set in a corner of the peaceful playing fields, with its trio of dormer windows on the top floor almost cloaked in ivy. Even the chimneys seemed extra tall, too. It was all impressive, enduring, permanent, secure: the perfect place to grow up, to remember with joy. Although almost palatial from the outside, it lacked many amenities, having cold stone passages all over the ground floor, and a generally dark air about it. But Rupert loved every crevice and seemed to be glad of its safety for the time being. Especially he loved the garden, part formal, part wilder. The whole situation, looking on to the playing fields called Big Side, was ideal.

Over on the left there rose the sharp strange outlines of a monkey-puzzle tree; beneath it, the fragrance of flowers at their late-July zenith; but best of all he liked the long grass path that he made his own by constant use. He would wander up and down its length, reading as he went. Old pergolas threaded overhead. And round to the right of School Field, he could see the Island – the large grass mound supporting the famous clump of trees that gave summer shade to the spectators of school games. For Rugby, remember, thrived on cricket and also gave its name to the brand

7

of football played with the hands as well as the feet. The game actually arose out of an incident in the autumn of 1823, on these very grounds, when one William Webb Ellis, while playing in the Close, caught the ball, but instead of retiring back and kicking it according to the rules of those times, had the extreme temerity to run with it clasped in his arms towards the opposing goal!

Rupert's fourteenth birthday passed and so did that summer when he was suspended between his preparatory school days and the Rugby years starting in September. He relished every high-summer day and realized that here was a turning-point in his life. The next would come exactly five years later as he left Rugby, but for the moment he stood on its threshold. Not only the threshold of Rugby, but the whole Edwardian decade which coincided with the start of the Michaelmas term.

While still at Hillbrow, Rupert had scribbled secretive verses; now with Rugby as stimulus and setting, he turned more toward this world. But at the same time, he had to accustom himself to the teeming, lunging life of 600 boys. In the process, he began to lose a lot of the introversion apparent when younger. He lived a normal school existence, but as always, he never became swamped by tradition or convention for their own sake. He could be impressed at the sense of solidity around him in the shape of big buildings; but he insisted rightly on ridiculing the incongruous castellations and giant Gothic excrescences of much of this monumental architecture. The rest accepted it, or more likely, never noticed it: Rupert questioned and commented.

For the first year or two, few of the boys in School Field realized that anyone out of the ordinary was among them. Rupert was still inclined to be quiet some of the time, though he could mix well, too, and proved himself good at games almost at once.

Although he lived much as anyone else, gradually they became aware of little differences about him. Instead of joining a group going 'down town', he went only as far as the newly-opened Temple Library.

Then he would call: 'Carry on and have a good time, you fellows, I've got to look at something over there'. He crossed the road with a wave, and vanished eagerly into the lofty single-storey structure to read the reviews of the latest books. Here he sat content, occasionally glancing up to the high, arched windows, and beyond to the trees on the Island. Books, and poetry in particular, were already in his essence.

H.F. Russell-Smith, one of the boys in the same house then, remembers him reading Walter Pater and other authors quite foreign to his companions. When he was not in the library, where even the tick of the clock in the corner echoed around the room, Rupert walked to and fro along his grass path, reciting the meter of a poem to the pounding of his step. Early in the century he discovered Oscar Wilde, Ernest Dowson and Swinburne. Rupert rhapsodized over Swinburne to his house friends who, on the whole, adopted an adamant indifference.

'The trouble is that you're all a lot of Philistines' he complained cheerfully.

His hair began to grow longer than was usual, and he won a school scholarship. But books did not exclude games. In his second summer, 1903, he played cricket for the House XI at an age younger than anyone else in the team, and later helped School Field to become Cock House in both football and cricket.

As Rugby and Rupert came to terms, he began to develop an extraordinary vitality, which showed itself in a boundless enthusiasm and boisterous sense of fun. When he wrote to his friends, too, this sense of the absurd was revealed in a kind burlesque of masters or boys, or parodies of himself.

Rupert usually seemed to be hurrying somewhere, when he was not studying. He and Russell-Smith used to dash across from School Field so as not to be late for chapel. Then after the day's work, another rush to Big Side prayers, when Rupert would sing the evening hymn at the top of his voice with a glorious disregard for tune.

One day when a sheep became entangled in one of the cricket nets, Rupert rushed on the Close to release the creature which was calling pitifully for help. But generally the boys saw him with a book, for while they were going for a walk or a bathe, he would be reading.

Rupert got through a great deal, but neither Rugby nor Cambridge persuaded him to pursue a steady scholastic course. He preferred to study what interested him most – seldom the conventional classics or the syllabus set! A little later, for instance, he wrote several chapters of an enormous romance, while he should have been busy with school work. So the Rugby scene was helping him to develop; but the things to spark his senses were the white moonlight strangely reflected on the glass roof of the observatory, or the huge elm beside the chapel, rather than the Greek epics.

By the time he was sixteen, Rupert was writing fluent adolescent verse, and in the spring of 1904 came his earliest recorded work, *The Pyramids*. This he composed for the annual prize poem for the school, and though it did not win, he received an additional award, as it was considered so nearly equal to the winning entry.

Imperfect and immature as it was, the poem promised much for the future, with lines like:

> And heard the roll and clangour of the years
> bearing on men and their little hopes and fears.

And later:

> Proud in the girdle of her Seven Hills,
> Indomitable Rome.

Perhaps the most promising mark was that he tried to avoid the cliché and the merely pretty phrase. In his original manuscript, one line read:

> child of the newborn France, the Corsican.

But when his mother had the poem privately printed in May 1904, he decided to change 'newborn' to 'newgrown'. Mrs Brooke, although she never for a moment understood her son properly, apparently recognized or realized that he had some talent by arranging for the poem to be circulated to their friends.

Three of his five years at Rugby had fled in the flurry of daily school routine. In the Michaelmas term, he saw himself in print for the first time more or less publicly. A touring company performed *As You Like It* in the Town Hall early in the term and Rupert contributed an unsigned notice of the play to the school magazine *The Meteor* on 1 November. Throughout the ten years left of his life, Rupert maintained a growing interest in the poetic theatre, most of all, the Elizabethan poet-playwrights.

The earliest examples of Rupert's poetry were contained in a second school publication, *The Phoenix*, which survived for only three numbers between 1904 and 1905. A prose offering entitled *A child's guide to Rugby School* showed he was no respecter of persons or place, but whether this could have been connected with the early demise of *The Phoenix* is not known! One of its successors, *The Vulture*, however, was definitely forbidden by the school authorities.

He initialled his more serious poems that winter 'E.R.T.' – the last three letters of his Christian name – and one of these, *The Return*, appeared in the next number of *The Phoenix*. This is the poem beginning:

Long had I dwelt in dreams and loneliness.

The others identified by the initials at this era were *Afterwards* and *In the End*, the latter remaining unpublished.

These early poems, scribbled in pencil in exercise books, convinced the strong-minded and puritanical Mrs Brooke that Rupert would benefit by travel. So during the Christmas holidays and the early part of the spring term, 1905, he spent some weeks in Italy and France, the first of numerous Continental excursions over the next six or seven years.

Rupert was reaching an educated adolescence, and about to embark on a phase of slight disillusion with the world. Real or assumed, this continued on and off for a couple of years or so, but was only a passing pose of youth. Anyway, he deigned to admire Botticelli, though expressing regret to find that the painter was in fashion with most people just then.

On this Italian trip, he was one of a party of thirty young Britons, mostly girls, and he actually enjoyed himself more than he admitted to his family. His cards home to them were brief in the extreme, but to his special school friends, with whom he now felt a closer link, he wrote at length on Italy and the arts. This 'disillusioned' spell was probably no more than a front to cover the transition from boyhood to man while values in general were tending to shift in consequence.

His intellect was awake. Now his emotions became conscious. At Fiesole, the party paused to discuss the merits of Browning, and then as the sun started to set westward of Florence, they watched the river Arno down in the distance, 'a writhing dragon of molten gold'.

These then were the formative years. He grew in mind and body; developed a natural charm with magnetic manner and features to match; and encouraged an innate sense of humour, which showed itself later in the whimsical undertones to much of his lyric poetry. Now, neither accurate nor studious in the accepted meanings, he preferred parodying a master to filling a notebook with lightly exotic – and erotic – fragments of verse.

By 1905 most traces of his former reticence had gone. He realized that poetry would be his profession, and he was discovering a burgeoning ability to express himself. Rupert still could not quite reconcile Rugby with his views on various things. But instead of rebellion, he favoured subtler means of overcoming the gulf between school and himself. He loved colour – and coloured ties. These were disallowed at school, but he cleverly got around the restriction by wearing large scarves at the neck of open-necked flannel shirts. This question of clothes might have seemed small and silly to some people, but to Rupert it became a matter of principle – though not ponderously so. He wanted the freedom to wear what he liked, just as later he felt the need to live as he liked. And in both cases, he managed to solve his dilemmas with a sly smile. It was no good being too serious about serious matters. But that did not mean he felt any less deeply about them. As far as clothes were concerned, the summer term came round again, and the need for formal suits relaxed.

Early in May, Rupert completed his second attempt for the prize poem, choosing as his subject *The Bastille*. When he heard he had won, he scampered down the stone passage of School Field to tell his mother, who was pleased yet still surprised at such an unlikely talent in a son of hers. And such strange ideas he had, too, she mused.

Rupert won a Browning and a Rossetti and had to recite the poem on Speech Day, 24 June. Fortified by the proximity of his friend, the musician Denis Browne, who sat at the piano for duty later in the proceedings, Rupert read:

Sullen athwart the freedom of the skies

12

It was clear he had progressed one year nearer to pure poetry.

The poem appeared in a publication for private distribution, in the pamphlet of prize compositions recited on that day in New Big School on the midsummer air, and also in the last issue of *The Vulture*.

Rupert's critical faculties were ripening, too, for he changed one or two lines in the printed version. Two other small alterations were the correction of the word 'irresistable' to '-ible', and the omission of a comma between the final two words

and Time Eternity.

Still we grope, he wrote, and the poet was in the throes of emerging, through the more mundane duties of the Cadet Corps and games.

A few days after school broke up in July, Rupert found himself standing stiffly to attention, his legs constricted in the puttees of his Rifle Corps uniform. He tried to ease each leg in turn, and cursed gently at such an uncomfortable uniform. Looking less debonair than usual, his khaki cap covered the mop of golden hair which seemed to be lightening by a tone each successive summer. The Cadet Corps went to the Public Schools' Camp for a strenuous, disciplined course. Rupert did his duty, but with the world in a slumbrous peace, it all seemed rather silly to him.

One of the first things he did the following term was to send a signed copy of *The Bastille* to St. J.B. Wynne Wilson, who had helped Rupert and quoted its last lines in his farewell sermon of the summer term before leaving Rugby for the headmastership of Haileybury.

He told Wynne Wilson of the passing of *The Phoenix* and *The Vulture*, adding that *The Venture* had just appeared. The aims of this were literary, Rupert assured him, but it included an article also on school football, so that the illiterates would be tempted into buying it and be educated unawares! The first issue in October published his poem *The Lost Lilies*.

Rupert started his last school year as a high-spirited intellectual eighteen-year-old, still subject to occasional bouts of reserve or remoteness. During the winter of 1905–06, he played the game which was almost a religion with the boys – rugby football – and gained a place in the First XV with this reference against his name:

R.C. Brooke (11st 12lbs.), a reliable centre three-quarter who, though not brilliant, is usually in his place, and makes good openings. He tackles too high.

Many times that winter, Rupert skidded fast towards the opposing goal-line, before passing out to his waiting wing three-quarters. He may not have been great at games, but the Rugbeians of the mid-Edwardian era remember him as a good man in a tight corner and one who could not stand slackers in a team. Even if he was not wildly keen on rugby, Rupert always tried hard.

By this time, most of the house had come under his spell. They accepted his interests, particularly since he was invariably so natural and took their chaff of his poetry as well. But it was his personal presence and charm that attracted them most; few could resist it.

During this school year, he was elected head of the house, and everyone under him was affected by his radiant personality. The spirit in School Field that year made the house different from any other, and was due to the two Brookes – father and son. The situation could easily have been awkward for both of them, but mainly because of Rupert's qualities, it never was for an instant. He remained loyal to his parent, while contriving not to make the rest of the house aware of his relationship with their housemaster. The secret lay in his immense sense of fun, for he never took any teacher very seriously. And the boys of School Field knew that they could rely on him never misinterpreting their attitude towards Mr Brooke.

Outside the house, Rupert's abilities became known and appreciated by the Upper Bench and a few of the specialized masters. He was in the sixth form now, and developing his debating powers at a series of society motions during the winter.

Five years had flown in a flash of poetic peace, traditional games, and the Rugby routine. Rupert was remembered 'with a ball in his hand and a book in his pocket'. The legend was unfolding. But he was never the school hero.

Just before Easter, 1906, he had an attack of ophthalmia. He and another senior were laid up in School Field as the sanatorium was full. A week went by without improvement to either of them, until Mr Brooke charged in as the family doctor was examining them

14

and told him that it was his fault. The two men's tempers rose, as Rupert and the other boy could only lie and listen. After this, they turned the corner and Rupert was packed off to Venice to recuperate for a fortnight. His eyes were better again there and he could see and sense the full magic, as he leaned over a bridge and watched his reflection softly stirring in the water below. Rupert was getting used to these changes of scene, and relied on them to widen his poetic powers.

Then back from Venice to the other Island, at Rugby, as late daffodils dotted the foot of the trees. Sitting sheltered and secure beneath their branches in the first week of the new term – his last at school – he finished off his English historical essay for the King's Medal for Prose. Its title read: 'England's Debt to William III'. Then, a characteristic afterthought, Rupert wrote: 'History repeats itself: Historians repeat one another'. Then he folded away the papers and went in to tea.

The essay holds no special significance, yet it won the medal with some ease. William III actually passed through Rugby on his way to fight the Irish in 1690. Now Rugby's only fame other than the school was as a railway junction and works. The twentieth century had dawned, but it was an era to which Rupert had already become completely committed.

The previous summer, his hair had only just started sprouting around the tight, white school cricket cap. Now it was longer and parted precisely in the middle, falling freely to either side. He revelled in his open shirts and self-striped sports trousers. Clad like this, he was photographed as one of the First XI, his legs crossed casually with confidence.

The last golden summer slipped away. The team went up to London for the annual match against Marlborough, whom they beat convincingly by 227 runs. It was an idyllic week, with Lords looking its midsummer greenest. Floral dresses were scattered colourfully around the ground, while parents and friends strolled over to the Tavern for a drink or snack.

Rugby batted first and scored 291. Rupert went in tenth, as he was being played for his bowling. He walked the long route out from the pavilion to the crease, and grinned at the Marlborough wicket-keeper, who had just made a catch. Five minutes later, he was walking back again for a duck! Marlborough replied with 231, and then the Rugby second innings came to a close at a declared score of 240 for 6 wickets. Rupert did not get another chance to bat. Marlborough were thus 300 runs behind, but in the last innings were routed for 73 all out. Rupert held a couple of catches at a vital stage in the match. The second was a hard, stinging chance which he caught with one hand. He had justified Rugby's memory of him as having 'a ball in his hand'. The last wicket fell at a quarter to six as the shadow of the pavilion was moving across the outfield. Suddenly it was all over – and the remaining few weeks of term cascaded from the calendar.

One of Rupert's house friends at School Field has said:

> I have always felt in myself that Rupert of all people at school gave me an inkling of what a full life really meant. He, with no appearance of superiority or attempt at preaching – as keen as any of us on all the immensely important events in school life and always ready for a rag – impressed us weaker brethren as no-one else could, with the fact that these things were not all, not even the most important. And the best thing about him was that he was not out to impress us.

Rupert looked with longing at Rugby that July, at all its oddly lovable buildings, where Samuel Butler, Matthew Arnold, Clough, Landor, and 'Lewis Carroll' had trod. He looked with sudden significance. It was all over. In *The Meteor* is his memory of it, as he recalled soon afterwards:

> I had been happier at Rugby than I can find words to say. As I looked back at five years I seemed to see almost every hour golden and radiant, and always increasing in beauty as I grew more conscious; and I could not and cannot hope for, or even quite imagine, such happiness elsewhere. And then I found the last days of all this slipping by me, and with them the faces and places and life I loved, and I without power to stay them. I became for the first time conscious of transience and parting, and a great many other things.

This same mood prompted him to write *The Farewell* later that year, a poem which ends:

But . . . the things we leave behind.
They are the best.

Appropriately his last act before leaving Rugby was to give a lecture devoted to modern poetry on his final Sunday at school. Neither muddled nor maudlin, this proved to be a lighthearted living hymn of praise for poetry in terms of the world around them: the world of Yeats and Dowson. Rupert always passionately preferred the art being created contemporarily apart from his love of John Donne and the Elizabethans.

Another summer holiday, and then from the spreadeagled silhouettes of familiar Rugby landmarks, he took a train to Bletchley and changed for Cambridge: a new skyline and a new life. He was nineteen, R.C. Brooke, freshman of King's College, a boy no more.

Chapter Two

Cambridge, the Carbonari and Poetry

As Brooke turned into King's Parade, with its famous facade of small-paned bookshop windows, and saw the stone college buildings in the pale amber afternoon, he suddenly experienced a wave of reticence and regret. He missed his old school friends, dispersed since the summer term ended, and he had yet to find fresh ones here. The lawns were beginning to lose their summer colour, and even the Backs at first sight seemed barren, the water dank and dark. Leaves curled aimlessly across the grass.

Undergraduates filled the pavement, moving and milling with just as little purpose. He shivered slightly as he walked into King's. It was all so strange. Here life had gone on for centuries already. But his own life at King's dated only from today, from this very moment when he walked past the porter's lodge and enquired after his rooms. Brooke felt fragile, alone.

Then he pulled himself together and found the rooms as an autumn mist was beginning to seep upstairs and cloud the gas-lights on the landing. After tea and toast, and with the lamps lit, things looked warmer, cosier, again. He unpacked his things and started sorting the little pile of books he had brought with him from Rugby. They did not fill the shelf provided, so he spaced them out a bit. Soon the room would be bulging with books, borrowed or bought, and the shelf be swamped with new-found favourites. This room was his immediate world. What lay beyond was hidden in the dusk, what lay ahead Brooke did not want to dwell on tonight.

He fell asleep that first night to the sound of the city's chimes from far and near, and when he awoke it was to the swelling sounds of a new term in a university college.

Still the strangeness lingered, though. Throughout his life, he had these occasional spells of deep depression, as if compensating for the intense level at which he lived. This one found expression in the 'decadent and disillusioned' pose, as practised at Rugby. He hung pictures by Aubrey Beardsley around his walls and began to keep eccentric hours to match – not recognizing any time before noon! There were actually a couple of other Rugby freshmen at the University, too, one of them Hugh Russell-Smith. Brooke sought out both these kindred souls, and also wrote mock laments to his friend St. John Lucas – another young 'decadent' – and to his cousin in Godalming, Erica Cotterill. All the people at Cambridge were too terribly clever and witty and wearying: this was the gist of his complaint. In fact, they were all growing up and revealing the familiar if necessary absurdities of young men. He lost interest in games, without the old loyalties of Rugby and School Field, disliked discipline as heartily as ever and still found imposed reading oddly onerous.

He alleged that he did not feel able to read or write to any purpose, yet in the first month or two at Cambridge he composed four recorded poems, including one early essay in the manner of 'ugliness' of which he was subsequently sometimes accused. *The Song of the Beasts* was the title and its lines contained this typical couplet:

> Though mad whispers woo you, and hot hands cling,
> And the touch and the smell of bare flesh sting.

Already, at nineteen, he was looking back on a girlfriend of Rugby days in another poem of the same season, *The Beginning*. Many times they had strolled by the banks of the Avon and stopped beside the still stream. This is more lyrical than *The Beasts* yet tinged with the regret he felt for those intimate, carefree years. The autumn mood of melancholy shows sadly in this little lyric:

> And I loved you before you were old and wise,
> When the flame of youth was strong in your eyes,
> – And my heart is sick with memories.

19

Brooke's introspection wore off as the term wore on. Strangely enough, he exchanged a paternal housemaster for an avuncular dean. His Uncle Brookie was Dean of King's then, so the family authority still lingered over him, if indirectly.

He met fresh fellow-spirits in King's. Not everyone was wearisome after all. On the first Sunday of the term, he ran into Hugh Dalton on the steps of the Provost Lodge, and the friendship which grew between these two was one of a number developed at Cambridge. Dalton went up to King's the same term as Brooke; he was exactly the same age, just twenty-three days younger; and he loved poetry as passionately. No Cambridge friendship meant more to Dalton than Brooke's over the next four years, and the relationship was reciprocal. Dalton possessed as great a feeling for fun then as half a century later, and was partly instrumental in helping Brooke over his first-term gloom.

Brooke could not enthuse over the syllabus, but nor could he repress for long his old joie de vivre, so as an outlet for it he branched into the dramatic field. His interest in poetic drama dated back several years already, and he persuaded the producer to give him a small part in the *Eumenides* of Aeschylus, played in the original Greek. He hoped to take the role of Hermes, but this went to someone more experienced, and he was left instead with the Herald in the final scene.

He was clad in classical dress of striking red, blue and gold, complete with wig, buskins, and clarion. His little band of friends sat spellbound in their seats as at the appointed second he appeared there in the midst of the proceedings, and raised the instrument to his lips with a flourish while the note really sounded off-stage. He was seen for only a minute or so, yet he looked as if he had stepped straight over the centuries from the ancient Hellenes. Arthur Benson, Master of Magdalene College, remembered that he seemed wholly without nerves. But although making a fine statuesque figure, dignified and self-possessed, Brooke monotoned his part in a Grecian chant without flexibility or dramatic sympathy! Perhaps he preferred his mother tongue, as his own verse was already proving essentially English. Another less favourable comment came in a review of the play which noted that 'a herald made a pretty figure spoilt by a glassy stare'.

Hardly an auspicious initiation. Brooke's only other venture that season was with the Cambridge Amateur Dramatic Company, playing a minor part in *She Stoops to Conquer*.

As an additional outlet in revolt against the dreary syllabus, Brooke and Dalton, with other equally staunch spirits, founded an exclusive little set christened the Carbonari, or charcoal burners, after an early-nineteenth century revolutionary society in liberty-seeking Italy. But belying its inflammatory name, the Carbonari held harmless meetings to read papers and poetry, and then discuss them. Arthur Waley, later an authority on Oriental poetry, was elected a member in his first year. He was then known by his real name of Schloss, which had to be changed to the more suitable surname of Waley during the next decade. War seemed unthinkable, though, in 1906. Some eight or nine others made up the group of a dozen, including Philip Noel-Baker and J. Steuart Wilson.

At one of their earliest meetings, Brooke read some of his poems to them. None had then been published, not even in Cambridge magazines to which he became an energetic contributor; in fact, one or two he read literally as the ink dried. More often they were scribbled illegibly in pencil on any scrap of paper about the room. This did not mean they were composed hurriedly, for he was always a careful craftsman. What he would be doing as he jotted down words just before reading to them was merely altering a phrase or filling in a blank word – a favourite finish of his.

The first time the Carbonari heard Rupert recite was something none of them forgot. The group were scattered casually in the shadowy folds of the room each focused on Brooke by the little lamp. The light caught the top of an occasional mug of beer and was reflected darkly. A few half-eaten hunks of cheese and slices of bread lay on plates. The evening was late. Outside, the weather cold.

Then he began to read, the light falling on his fair hair. The combined sense of the poem and Brooke's voice moved Dalton deeply as he listened amazed at their imagery and music. Most of them felt the same. Dalton knew he could create poetry, but until this instant in a room at King's College, he had no idea of the full beauty. Brooke read verse in a small group far better than anyone Dalton had ever heard, with his flowing rhythm, perfect stress, and sense of drama. When Brooke finished a poem, a moment's quiet prolonged the mood before a murmur of male voices applauded the lines just faded from the air. These were the moments which Brooke was later able to suspend and recapture in whole poems. Now, however, they were *The Vision of the Archangels*, *Day that I have Loved* and *The Beginning* that were the best of this juvenilia, which was still inevitably immature yet remarkable for its promise. These three were Dalton's own favourites from the period, and his roguish features sharpened in anticipation as he heard Brooke begin them on those winter nights. The kind of nights at the time of their lives which would stay with them as impressions of the whole meaning of their early Cambridge years, when life was young and they were eager to meet it.

Reciting poetry in a larger gathering, Brooke sounded less effective and Russell-Smith and Dalton both beat him at a later date to win the Winchester reading prize for the particular years. This loss of quality could be compared with his acting ability, which was much more vital in the relaxed and intimate circle of a rehearsal than at the actual performance.

Meanwhile, Brooke began to lose his autumn nostalgia for the green playing fields of Rugby, his personal grass path, and those architectural absurdities. He and Dalton talked modern poetry much of their spare time. Both came to Cambridge rather drunk with Swinburne. Now they felt it was time to grow up and move on, towards the fresh fields of Housman's *Shropshire Lad*, for instance, which they read to each other in their rooms to get the full effect. As Dalton said: 'We went into the Celtic Twilight with the early Yeats and stayed to see Synge's plays acted as the daylight grew.' Then Brooke put Dalton on to Hilaire Belloc, who was later to materialize miraculously before them, larger than life.

Another writer, of a different sort, whom they hero-worshipped, was Charles Masterman. They thought of him as the young leader of the Radical-Socialist wing of the Liberal Party. Brooke belonged to no political party or society yet, but ever since that pro-Boer demonstration, he clearly held radical views. Before he left home, he had helped the Liberals locally in the 1906 general election, editing an election paper which appeared on alternate days, and canvassing all and sundry in respectable Rugby. This was mainly just for the fun of it, however, rather than a reflection of political awareness.

Hugh Dalton joined the Fabian Society as soon as he reached

Cambridge, but Brooke was still in the embryonic stage, and more interested in the arts than politics.

So on and off for the rest of the term, Brooke continued playing the 'modern decadent', languishing with copies of Verlaine and Baudelaire, decking his study with green rugs and curtains to match the mood of his Beardsley sketches! He told his friend St. John Lucas that he wanted to complete his set of books by those three decadents – Wilde, Lucas and Brooke! He added that he had given up writing for the moment, as there were only ten beautiful words in the English language and he had used them all. He had already written of love too much.

So the term went on till Christmas came, when he fell ill. A friend, Gertrude Lindsay, came round to School Field several times to draw a portrait of him, otherwise nothing happened, he complained. Idleness and indifference irritated him even more than enforced study of the dead classics. For all he wanted to do was to read poetry, write poetry, and best of all to live poetry, as he announced to Dalton on one famous occasion.

'As you know, Hugh,' Brooke added softly, 'At rare moments, I have glimpses of what poetry really means, how it solves all problems of conduct , settles all questions of values.'

It was more in this frame of mind that he returned after the vacation. Then almost at once, the first real sorrow of his life swept aside all self-absorption. His older brother, Dick, who had always looked frail, suddenly died on 13 January 1907. Brooke received the news in his study the next day, and automatically returned to Rugby to try and comfort his mother, ill with the shock of it. After he had done all he could, he retraced the journey he made only a week earlier to Cambridge.

He wanted to be alone; not even with Dalton; completely alone. This did much to shake him out of the immature 'decadence' of the previous term, but it seemed a high price to pay. He walked around the town, through the bustling market, explored strange parts away from King's, then found himself along the Backs. Pastel sunlight filtered from the January sky, as he leaned over a bridge and looked abstractedly down at the water. Dick was dead. What did it mean? Why had it happened? They were not especially close, but they had been brothers. So there was something deep in the blood after all. Strange, he thought, how two people can be apart in space and outlook yet be linked like this by the family tie. Dick, Dick; Brooke thought back to their years at home and unconsciously tried to visualize his face, and what they had done together. All he could see was a composite across the years; Dick as a boy, a youth, a man, and now no more.

He threw a loose stone from the bridge into the water, and saw his own image in the water shattered into a rippling circle. He walked back to his study.

Rupert still had no time for the Church, but he could not resist stealing into the great Chapel at King's one afternoon, whose four fingers of Gothic carved stone pointed high to heaven from each corner.

As he moved inside, the late sun came out, and at the same second Bach was wafted on to the air from the organ overhead. Filtered sound and sun filled the vast vault of glass, stone and wood. Then a chord throbbed through the building, and an elation surged, swept, into Brooke's body. The notes ended, yet the strength of their sound still hung in the air.

He looked up at the amazing arcs of stone spanning the roof. Eighty feet above him, a fine fretwork of stone had stood there suspended for four and a half centuries, interlaced, splaying from the tall walls. His eyes moved down these walls to the rich red and blue of the windows, their slender elegance emphasized in groups of four. Here was peace, apart from any feeling for religion. Peace and wonder, that here it had stood since 1450.

A dramatic division, the deep brown wood organ, with its gold pipes gleaming and pointing high, and the figures of heralds atop the organ, their trumpets gold, too.

Rupert walked down the aisle, under the huge organ loft, as a shadowy silhouette was lighting the choristers' candles, in pairs and singly, behind their protective glass. He saw the low, late sun fall across clusters of candles around the altar, then the great glass window above it; red, blue and green glass towering toward the roof. He stood there some time, turned, and walked slowly back and out into the air again. The sun was setting round to the right behind the Backs. Life seemed strange and wonderful.

Brooke determined to occupy his mind to the limit after the first few days back, and flung himself into a furore of activity, including the ultimate ignominy – reviewing minor poetry for the university's *Cambridge Review*!

Before he had got as far as opening the first of seven dreary volumes of verse sent for comment, he heard that he had won a prize in one of the *Westminster Gazette*'s weekly literary competitions. His entry appeared on 2 February, and a comment on it followed only five days later in the *Cambridge Review* which wrote:

'Once more it is encumbent upon us to congratulate a competitor for the prizes offered in the Westminster Gazette. It is said that Brooke was successful with a translation from German to English verse; and we understand that it is the Freshman of that name, rather than the Dean, whose efforts have received appreciation.

The very next week, the *Review* published his poem *The Call* which he later thought worth preserving in volume form. It reflected a love of life, proper in someone still under twenty and, like this young life, its poetry was not yet clarified or controlled. Not that Brooke ever came to terms with life completely, which was probably as well, or he might not have been urged on by the compulsion of conflict. Already he had the force to appreciate beauty:

> I'll write upon the shrinking skies
> The scarlet splendour of your name.

With this sense of the joyous, and an almost exaggerated realism, would come qualities of impishness, imagination, and controlled passion.

Next he proceeded to deal dispassionately with the six unlucky poets sent for review. One of them had actually produced two volumes of verse, accounting for seven in all. Brooke sat in his study on the gloom-grey of a February afternoon reading each one conscientiously, lost to the outer world, and then wrote a short critical note covering all half-dozen. As this was to appear on 28 February, he headed the article *Et toute la reste. . .* a playful aside at the date and a polite damnation of poets who had composed such pretententious pieces as *The New Crusade*. The same day as these reviews appeared, the *Westminster Gazette* published a prose poem *The Five Knights*, his first publicly published verse.

Mr and Mrs Brooke still grieved deeply over their eldest son's death, and when Rupert went home the next few times he took care to be even more cheerful than usual, though he had felt the loss as much as them. In his letters to his cousin Erica, he said that he was puzzled about it all, felt tired and old, and did not believe in God. But he did believe in life infinitely more than most people.

With his dramatic and Carbonari activities firmly rooted, Brooke blossomed as a Fabian, too. In April, he waylaid Hugh Dalton, to try and convey his feelings: 'I'm not your sort of socialist' he said with a twinkle, 'I'm a William Morris sort of socialist, but I want to join your society as an associate – if you'll have me.' This was the Cambridge University Fabian Society, and Dalton said yes.

In an unpublished poem of this precise period, now probably lost, Brooke hoped for a better world, where all men should share a larger life:

> lest man go down into the dark
> with his best songs unsung.

Dalton kept a record of these lines. Almost from their first meeting, he realized that Brooke was no ordinary freshman, and he preserved all the letters, postcards and manuscripts from Rupert, feeling them to be important .

In view of his Liberal – and Labour – leanings, Brooke's interest in the Fabians came as only logical. The fact that he had likened himself to the outlook of Morris was also in character, for he felt most concerned for the creative artist, and would never conform to a doctrine merely to fall in line; rather the reverse.

All this time, too, he continued to emerge as a radiant and remarkable pensonality.

Fabianism was indirectly responsible for him meeting the four Olivier sisters, all of whom he liked. Their father, Sydney Olivier, came over to speak from Oxford, and at a supper party afterwards, Brooke was introduced to the four girls – Marjery, Daphne, Bryn and Noel. It was Noel who fell under his spell most of all, though their friendship did not develop until the following year or so, as she was only an adolescent in 1907. Even at that age, the memory of the fair-haired man at that Cambridge supper haunted her. Rupert was dazzling as he pressed the girls to plates of food and hot drinks. At this particular supper in the rooms of Ben Keeling, Noel Olivier was actually less than sixteen and still at the celebrated co-educational school of Bedales in Petersfield, Hampshire. During the following few years, Rupert and Noel met many times, both in public and in secret. Later on, too, he proposed to her. . .

He entered for a couple more contests in the *Gazette* during May and June, but although his attempts were printed, neither received the prize. Then two further fragments appeared in July, one winning the prize. It was for the completion of a poem, and the judges all agreed that Brooke's entry was distinctly better than the opening portion of the poem set to be finished!

Summer saw four more poems published at Cambridge under his 'scarlet spell'. After the scarlet splendour in *The Call* two contained reference more to this colour:

My song, a flame of scarlet, on your brows.

This was from *My Song*, one of three poems in the June 1907 book of King's, the *Basileon*. It was coupled with *Dawn* and *The Wayfarers*, the latter including the lines:

Will pale a little your scarlet lips, each mile
Dull the dear pain of your remembered face.

His down-to-earth realism appeared in *The Dawn*, written in a second-class train compartment between Bologna and Milan, while returning home from Venice the previous year.

Opposite me two Germans snore and sweat
Through sullen swirling gloom we jolt and roar.

Throughout this first year at Cambridge, he wrote dozens, probably hundreds, of poems, and then burnt most of them as soon as they were composed, or after he had read them to someone.

At the end of the May term the most significant event before Brooke left on his holiday was his first meeting with Eddie Marsh. The patron from Whitehall soon saw that the poet was, in Frances Cornford's words, 'magnificently unprepared' for the humdrum life. But their friendship had to wait, for Brooke was about to leave

27

for Lulworth in Dorset, with other friends. Here he lazed among the rocks and rippling waters of the Cove, and thought things rather dull as he complained of a lack of promenade and pier: nothing but the green arcs of Dorset downs sweeping to sheer white cliffs. And although he was declaring as usual that he was writing nothing, towards evening on 8 July, he was stirred by the sight of pine trees silhouetted after sunset:

> Very beautiful, and still, and bending over
> Their sharp black heads against a quiet sky.

He was happy and laughed and no longer wished to die. The poem reflected exactly his feelings at that time: the gradual eclipse of the era of 'decadence' and a move towards a freer, frank, if emotional, approach to life. Brooke hummed a song out of tune as he strode down to the village in the light of the summer moon that night. And the scent of the pines followed him as he went.

The sea was encouraging a love of swimming, not one of his main interests before now, but becoming a passion in the later, Grantchester days. Next term, too, he resumed organized games, though not quite with wholehearted zeal. But now it was still summer, Edwardian summer, with the drowsy sound of the sea, the lull of Lulworth.

For the lack of much else to do, Brooke read his syllabus classics, and wrote and read poems. One day perched on some rocks a copy of Keats fell out of his pocket and was swept to sea by the currents scurrying around the rocks. Brooke and a friend hopped onto a rowing boat and tracked the book down the coast, till they caught it being bruised against other rocks. Brooke retrieved the volume with difficulty, but it was none the less ruined.

Years later, he discovered that by an amazing coincidence Lulworth had been the last land Keats had trodden before leaving Britain forever. In September 1820, his becalmed ship stood-by outside Lulworth waiting for a wind. Keats went ashore with Joseph Severn for the day and clambered among those same rocks, before returning to the *Maria Crowther* to sail for Italy. Back aboard, he wrote his last sonnet starting:

> Bright star! Would I were steadfast as thou art –

A year later he was dead.

For Keats, Lulworth meant the last of England; to Brooke, it became a point from which he began to find himself. Despite the front of exaggerated ennui he liked to present in his letters, such as the one on attaining his twentieth birthday which had plunged him into despondency, this attitude was now not much more than a facade. Preciosities were past. Enthusiasm for life was winning over languorous cynicism. But all was not calm, for the spirit of Brooke burned too bright with ecstasy to be maintained at such a pitch permanently. Meanwhile, he went back to Cambridge, and the first thing he did at college was to play football.

Chapter Three

Hugh Dalton, and Rupert reaches Twenty-One

Life throbbed through King's and Cambridge that autumn at an exciting, vibrant pace. The young don Bertrand Russell remembered that they were a lively group at the University during those vintage years. Rupert no longer resented the place or regretted Rugby, where every hour had been golden; in fact, he developed naturally as a pivot or prominent member of every group he joined.

His legendary circle of friends began to form, for he had an unconscious talent for attracting staunch people around him. Dalton, Eddie Marsh (only occasionally seen), the Olivier girls, Frances Cornford, Geoffrey Keynes, Reginald Pole. The list was to multiply before long; now he stood on the brink of the crowded years. Brooke knew Keynes from earliest Rugby days, and it was he who helped Rupert at Cambridge with translations for the contests in the *Westminster Gazette*. Keynes also assisted by saving all his press-cuttings and contributions to periodicals, so already Keynes and Dalton were aware of his worth.

Brooke had a clear impact on Reginald Pole, who found him one of the few utterly real and rare personalities he had ever met. Pole had never known a poet to match him for simple, unaffected communication of truth, unashamed as he was of every emotion that might ripple over the surface of his mind.

This personality observed by Pole was beginning to have a vitalising effect on the Carbonari, Fabians, the philosophic Apostles, the Heretics, and other societies. Yet above all other activities this term, it was drama that absorbed him most apart from pure poetry.

Dr Edward Dent, professor of music, noticed too that on his return to Cambridge after the long vacation of 1907, a new spirit seemed to be stirring there. He decided that it emanated from Rugby and Bedales. The two leaders were both, by coincidence, called Brooke: Justin Brooke hailed from Bedales, that progressive Hampshire school, and Rupert from Rugby. They were not related.

Justin, three years the elder, formed an acting group soon after term started and went along to see Rupert one evening to tell him about it.

'I remember you were in the Eumenides last year, Rupert, and seem to be keen on the theatre, so I wonder if you'd care to be a member of this new group of ours?'

'Care to? I'd love it.'

Between them they settled on a play to launch the group: Marlowe's *Faustus*.

'Well, what shall we call ourselves?' Justin thought, 'How about the Marlowe Dramatic Society?'

The fact that Christopher Marlowe had himself been at Cambridge until 1587 appealed to Rupert, with his passion for the Elizabethan drama, and so he agreed to the title as eagerly as he accepted the invitation. Marlowe blew life, strength, and everything else into tragedy, Rupert believed, and he admired the dramatist's love of the body, his passion for the world of colour and stuff, his glorious atheism.

Like all else he ever entered into, Rupert devoted his whole being to the play. When considering the casting, someone said:

'Wouldn't Rupert be right for the part of Helen?'

This was followed by a deep discussion among the rest, but in the end they saw him for some reason in the darker devilry of Mephistopheles, a role as far out of character as could be conceived.

A series of secretive, but excitedly enthusiastic rehearsals prepared them for the performance in the A.D.C. Theatre of the university. The mid-Edwardian audience settled into their seats after their evening meals, and looked at the programme. No names of actors appeared. An uneasy buzz of conversation went round the stalls. That was the first shock. Many more were to follow; things that seemed extra startling against the comfortingly familiar setting

31

of the theatre, with its portraits of past personages all around the walls.

The chatter finally died down as the curtains parted on that November night. Then the older members of the audience gasped, the younger ones sat up straighter. For they saw no footlights, no scenery, nothing but a general green gloom engendered by dark velvet curtains. There was no incidental music as atmosphere. The conventional among the audience assumed a state of scandalized astonishment at the entire evening, which was admittedly unusual. Behind the stage, the cast waited pent up, and Rupert made last-minute adjustments to his cowl.

Dr Dent agreed that it was indeed a queer performance. Faustus looked absurdly young; the devil (Rupert), his face completely hidden by his cowl, generally turned his back on the audience, and spoke in a thick, indistinct voice. But in spite of these things, and the tedious humour of the comic scenes, the play really did have a new spirit all of its own. The tragic moments were genuinely moving. Crude, awkward, and amateurish as it was, the spirit of true poetry shone through, and those of the audience responsive to the idea felt that to these actors poetry was the greatest thing in life.

This, then, explained much of the reasoning behind the revolutionary staging. The group wanted to paint an impression in poetry, and to do so discarded all distractions such as scenery and music. The mood and the words were all.

But the stupefied spectators were not really impressed. This was Edwardian, not Elizabethan, England. Play presentation had 'progressed' since then. The comments in the intervals and after-wards confirmed their reaction:

'*Faustus* isn't a play at all' the elderly said, shaking their heads, 'and anyway, it was absurd for undergraduates to attempt tragedy.'

'If they were really set on it, why didn't they get somebody with experience to coach them?'

'Why do they act in the dark?'

The questions volleyed out into the night, the final words echoing distantly down the still street: 'It wasn't always in very nice taste, was it, my dear?' The crowning condemnation.

'*Faustus*' had been different, so it must be wrong. But Dr Dent and a few others saw its sincerity and he made his way backstage at the end to find the two Brookes.

32

'Don't worry, it had poetry and art' he told them.

'That's not what the audience thought' Rupert said.

'Never mind, you stick to your ideas and keep in touch with me. I'll expect to see something else from you soon.'

Rupert had handled the poetic passages with the true feeling to be expected, but the more dramatic moments proved beyond him, and he was conscious of this as he changed from his black costume.

'He had no essentially histrionic gift, but he delivered poetry quite beautifully' Reginald Pole wrote. Yet if Brooke's ability on stage lacked drama, the production as a whole owed a lot to his imagination behind the scenes. His forte was clearly creative rather than interpretative, but he could not help wringing any poetry out of a printed page.

While rehearsing for *Faustus*, Brooke did not neglect poetry, politics or the Carbonari, which added a few freshmen in October. In fact, his own outlook on the relationship between economics and the arts was actually voiced in a public lecture during November by H. Granville Barker on Socialism and the Drama. Brooke listened to this rapt, and reported its main points for the local newspaper.

Among Granville-Barker's points were that if you 'look after the economics, the art will come of itself'. As far as Brooke was concerned, this applied to poetry, painting and all the arts just as it did to drama, and three years later almost to the day he developed his own imaginative ideas in a lecture to the Cambridge Union Fabian Society.

George Bernard Shaw visited the Fabians the same week as Granville-Barker was in the town, and roused most of them there to a pitch of extreme enthusiasm with his Irish wit and passion. But Brooke had yet to be convinced that he felt sufficiently in sympathy to accept the doctrines fully. Too much stress seemed to be laid on material, selfish and partisan ends, too little on pure idealism. He still saw some goodness in people politically opposed to him, and he retained more tolerance of the existing order than most Fabians. Yet this was the world of the young Shaw, Wells and the Webbs, and he felt just as fervently in favour of some sort of change from the competitive, top-heavy social structure. He was probably closest in view to his uncle, Erica's father, Clement Cotterill, who had just finished a social study 'Human justice for those at the

Bottom from those at the Top!' Cotterill sent his nephew a copy of it in November, and he reviewed it on publication the following May.

Wedged in amid all these activities, themselves additional to the curriculum, Brooke read and autographed in November a book by John C. Bailey on *The Claims of French Poetry*. He furthered his acquaintance with Marot, Ronsard, La Fontaine, André Chenier, Hugo and De Lisle. This term seemed so crowded that Brooke found few days for composing verse of his own. And anything he did write, he could not have considered of value, for nothing was published or survives.

Another New Year and by mid-January, Brooke was reviewing more verse and composing an occasional sonnet. One in a light vein, that month, started:

This thing must end, I am no boy!

It proceeded as a lighthearted fourteen lines of revolt on reaching the age of twenty-one, which he was due to do shortly. This he followed a fortnight later in the *Cambridge Review* with a poem inspired by a moment that he managed to suspend, analyse and record, before it dissolved. As if the world were halted for just that space of a second. It was *In examination* when the sun suddenly streamed in through the window of a King's room, and:

To the left and to the right,
Hunched figures and old
Dull blear-eyed scribbling fools, grew fair,
Ringed round and haloed with holy light.

The vision lasted till the light faded and they were grey again. An intriguing difference is revealed here between the date of the published poem, 20 February, and that ascribed to it in the Collected Poems – 18 November the same year.

Meanwhile, like a magnet, Brooke drew around him an ever widening charmed circle of men and women, and his mind widenened with it. He took people as they came, and refused to be impressed by reputations. Thomas Hardy had just completed his monumental blank-verse portrayal of the Napoleonic Wars, *The*

Dynasts, when Brooke ate breakfast with him one day. But Rupert was very disappointed in him, for he had a thin and pessimistic voice behind a heavy moustache: a voice intoning at the inferior toast and about little else! When Brooke met Dalton and the rest next time, he told them of this depressing soliloquy on toast and things unliterary.

'We won't toast Hardy, then,' a wag piped up.

The Carbonari continued to burn their charcoal at both ends. Brooke, Dalton, and one or two others were generally the last to separate, often with the dawn in the sky beyond the gates of the college. Rupert would still read his latest poems to them or they would try to thrash out the whys and woes of the world, meeting in each others' rooms.

Rupert's room, especially, had grown to mean the Carbonari meetings, for here they had their happiest nights. One particular evening they recalled from the many. Squat, intimate and sprinkled with books, the room had a lamp hanging from the ceiling, which swung slightly on the early-spring night breeze, blown via the narrow door or a window left ajar. Through one of these, too, were wafted an elusive assortment of scents and sounds from the meadows and river.

Brooke rushed around among the group, providing them with the wholesome if frugal fare of beer, bread and cheese. The excitement was rising now, for one of their current heroes had accepted their invitation. Suddenly Rupert shouted:

'Quiet – listen. Someone on the stairs.'

And the next moment, the door was pushed dramatically into the room, and there framed in it against the darkness stood the form of Hilaire Belloc.

'Welcome to the Carbonari' Brooke called, extending a hand. And that was the signal for the start of a scintillating evening. Everyone seemed at their wittiest and four hours flashed past in an instant. Then as the great man finally left for his own room after midnight, Brooke said: 'Do come along here for breakfast if you'd like.' Belloc accepted.

After an evening like that, Brooke was inclined to sleep on a bit the next morning, and the following day the habit did not change. About half-past nine, he stirred finally and saw the breakfast set in motion, then he vanished to tidy up with one of his infrequent shaves. In passing, he left the front door open in case anyone arrived.

Ten minutes later, Belloc strode in and with a couple of heavy steps stood towering over the frying pan in the living room, where eggs and bacon were spitting away merrily. At that moment, Brooke entered from the bedroom, Dalton through the front door, and both of them found him sniffing the pan with a ponderous look of doubt, if not disgust!

'Don't you feel like eggs and bacon?' Rupert asked anxiously. 'If there's anything you'd rather have—'

'This will be admirable' said Belloc slowly, 'but first I'd love a tankard of audit ale!'

Brooke and Dalton breathed out explosively, the beer was at once summoned, Belloc duly drained it, and then they all sat down to breakfast, Belloc's seat tending to overlap the modest dimensions of the dining chair.

Inspired by this visit, Brooke read a paper on Belloc to the Carbonari, complete with quotations.

On their occasional all-night sessions, a few of them would walk round the courts and beside the river for hours, trying to get life clear. For they wanted, half passionately, half humorously, to sort it all out quickly. Until then, they imagined, they had been too young to think seriously; soon they might be too busy; ultimately, too old. The golden time was now, and they were aware of an awakening urgency as they strolled the paths surrounding the Backs, while the moonlight threw soft shadows over the grass; half a dozen young men seeking their own answers to the eternals.

To read poetry, write poetry, live poetry – Brooke's philosophy would keep men young always, he thought. One night, he and Dalton were sitting at a high window overlooking King's Parade. They had been discussing some point about the nature of beauty, when they saw and heard some drunken members of another college going home.

Quickly Brooke said: 'Those fellows would think us very old if they had been in this room tonight, but when they go down and sit on office stools, they will grow old quite suddenly, and many years hence we shall still be talking and thinking about this sort of thing, and we shall still be young.

So there was time after all, as long as they never forgot the poetry and the wonder, and avoided becoming immersed in the deadly routine of the world.

Brooke spoke with his usual infectious enthusiasm, however apparently arid the topic. Although the eternal issues might seem dry to the drunken undergraduates reeling along King's Parade, he always knew that these were what really mattered most.

Rupert shared the general view of their set that it mattered immensely what was good, but comparatively little what was real. He had several fierce arguments with Dalton as to whether a man's character, as distinct from the series of states of mind through which he passed, could be good in itself; and also a controversy as to whether states of affairs, as distinct from states of mind of the persons concerned in them, could be good in themselves.

Rupert maintained that variety was good in itself. 'A world containing you and me and Maynard Keynes' he told Dalton one day, 'is obviously better than a world containing three people exactly like any of us.' Maynard Keynes was afterwards the distinguished economist.

But Brooke never suppressed his humour, however philosophic the subject, and he was always aware of the ironic in life.

'His effervescent élan always made me feel happier' Dalton told me; 'reading his letters one could almost hear him talking. And his poetry flowed forth just like live conversation – it was not forced into any special mould.'

Throughout the term, Brooke persevered with his attitude to the arts, propounding to the Fabians the need for artists of promise to be assured of food, fuel and clothes for their work to proceed without waste of effort worrying over basic livelihood. Brooke was convinced that art did not flourish in adversity, so it was up to society to see that poor but promising people were encouraged. The Fabians were interested, but their main concern lay with the living conditions of the majority, and they were less immediately absorbed with the fate of future artists.

Nevertheless, despite any difference he had with them over emphasis for social reform, he finally felt close enough to their outlooks to apply for full membership. His decision was hastened by talks that spring with H.G. Wells, when the visionary Fabian visited Cambridge. Brooke made up his mind in the Easter vacation

of 1908 on the way to Torquay, and told Dalton of it in a postcard
from that respectable resort immediately on arrival:

April 8th, 1908 (and for 10 days)
at 3 Beacon Terrace
Torquay!

Dear Hugh,
"Under the influence of a) talks with the wee fantastic Wells
b) his books c) Fabian tracts d) Private meditation and
prayer e) Arguments on the other side f-z) anything, etc, I
have decided to sign even the present Fabian Basis, and to
become a member (if possible) of the Central Fabian Society.
The former part, I suppose, may wait till next term; as I have
no Basis with me. Spiritually, the thing is done (not without
blood and tears). But the latter – is it possible? What steps can
I take, even now? Where write? What say? . . . Tell me . . . I
am eager as a neophyte always is, for action."
Yours
R

Dalton was quite delighted to receive this. Like many of them,
Brooke was falling by then under the subtle influence of the Webbs,
and simultaneously the atmosphere of Cambridge was teaching
him to value and to cultivate lucidity of thought and precision of
reasoning. Dalton was glad that he had seen the intellectual
limitations of a 'William Morris sort of socialist' and although
Rupert never studied the fine points of economics, he came to talk
very good sense on the larger economic questions.
    Spring came early as always to the subtropic Torquay plant life,
and Rupert basked in its haze of blossom and glossy leaves and
after dark he looked out past the little coloured boats in harbour
to the faint, flickering lights tracing the coastline to Brixham and
beyond. April in Devon, a beautiful, bitter-sweet time, with the
spring sun lighting red earth, fawn sand, and the sweep of the sea
round the bay.
    Then back to the buzz and bustle of Cambridge in late April with
bicycles beginning to make the market square incredibly full.
    The editor of the *Cambridge Review* came to Brooke for a poem

to help fill the first number of the new term. He supplied *On the death of Ta-Urt, the Hippopotamus Goddess*. Ta-Urt was re-christened Smet-Smet in the Poems of 1911.

Brooke's worth was becoming known outside the gates of King's, and around this time he received an invitation to join the Apostles, a group which met once a week to discuss philosophic subjects in a not-too-stuffy way. The society was formed in 1820 – the year of Keats at Lulworth – and only one or two promising people were elected to it each year, so it represented an honour. Bertrand Russell, fifteen years older than Brooke, Lytton Strachey, and other prominent personalities were members, and it was actually at the suggestion of Lowes Dickinson that Brooke's name had been included for election. Bertrand Russell first met Brooke through the Apostles and liked his company, recalling that he was 'loads of fun'. Russell told me this over tea and toast in his London home near the Tate Gallery.

Brooke was busier than ever this May, when his sonnet *Failure* was published . In June, the *Cambridge Review* printed *Pine-Trees and The Sky*: *Evening* written at Lulworth the previous summer. To the *Basileon* for June he contributed *Seaside*. This was probably Torquay with its reference to 'the friendly lilt of the band'. Here, as in another work of the period, are occasional lines of beauty which grow more frequent as he begins to master the currency of poetry. For example:

The sullen waters swell towards the moon.

But Brooke was occupied more with applied poetry for the rest of the term: the poetry of Milton's *Comus*. Brooke cherished a hope of producing it ever since *Faustus*, and he discovered the perfect excuse for performing it in 1908 – the great poet's tercentenary. Milton had studied at Christ's College and so the university intended to celebrate the year. What could be more fitting than for the Marlowe Society to give *Comus* dating from the poet's youth in 1634? Although *Faustus* had not impressed the authorities, they relented enough to consent to *Comus* being staged, even en-couraging it.

Brooke greeted the news with wild delight, throwing a book he had been reading up to the ceiling. At once he took on the first of many tasks in connection with the performance, becoming in fact the core of the company. He repaired to room Theta of the University Library practically every day, to study books on theatre construction. Moreover, he was determined to be just to Milton's memory, procuring the Trinity facsimile manuscript copy of *Comus*, to compare it with published versions for textual purity.

The group grew to include Frances Darwin (later Frances Cornford) and her cousin Gwen Darwin (later Gwen Raverat), and several girls of Newnham College taking part for the first time. Brooke's charm and candour, coupled with his appearance, appealed to practically all the girls; Newnhamites, as they were known.

After he had approved the final text, he became immersed in innumerable details. As artistic director of the project, he discussed with Justin Brooke ideas for costumes, and then went on to evolve effects in scenery à l'avant garde Gordon Craig. For days before the play, Brooke helped Albert Rutherston, the artist actually painting the scenes, by fetching pails, filling paint-pots, and in between times, supervising the direction and movement of the play, which involved also menial tasks like winding pulleys. Ultimately he created some wonderful settings, using such devices as scaffold poles placed in unusual ways.

Rupert was entirely happy for a week or two, perhaps for the first time since coming to Cambridge. It was all he could do to cope with the flow of fresh jobs. He always craved for new experiences, people and places as long as he lived, and savoured them all so deeply that he was exhausted before exhausting them.

With the men all about twenty to twenty-two, and a group of girls to help, everyone revelled in the work. And through it all shone the indefinable esprit of Brooke, daubing paint on the forest trees, reciting his lines lyrically, flirting with the girls. One of his helpers was Noel Olivier, now very attracted to him. One girl from the *Comus* production played with him in *The Importance of Being Earnest* and he wrote to his cousin that she was very beautiful and nice and everything. And every evening they rehearsed and he had to make love to her all the time!

But *Comus* proved more demanding than this, and Rupert used his entire resources on it. They rehearsed at every odd hour they could, either in the theatre or on the lawn of a neatly walled garden with a solid summerhouse in the corner. Rupert was taking his part of the Attendant Spirit, or else coaching one or more of the others. There in this old English garden, the clock slipped back three centuries as they stalked about in seventeenth century clothes, and Milton's words hung on the heavy summer air, until a girl's sudden laugh brought them back to reality and the modern life of 1908, with university students of both sexes audaciously acting together.

At last the rehearsals were over and it was the night of the play. Brooke's settings were remarkable, and his own portrayal more satisfactory than in *Faustus*. Dr Dent had been following their progress with interest and, from what he had glimpsed of rehearsals, took his seat expectantly. He knew, too, of course, that here was to be a play of more importance to the life and growth of the participants than the audience: a work of their art and self-expression. Here is how he described the occasion:

'It is difficult to criticise *Comus*, or to write a history of its preparation. It had much the same faults and the same merits as *Faustus*, though on a larger scale. . . Yet I feel now that anyone who remembers *Comus*, and remembers it with ever so slight a sense of beauty, will think of Rupert as the central figure of it; and watching rehearsals daily, as I did, I felt that, however much his personal beauty might count for, it was his passionate devotion to the spirit of poetry that really gave *Comus* its peculiar and indescribable atmosphere.

Comus, however unimportant to the world at large, did, in fact, mean a great deal for Rupert and his friends. It was the first time that he had! had to bear the responsibility of a large undertaking and he addressed himself to it in the spirit of a scholar. It deepened his sense of poetry, of drama, and of music; it made him develop an ideal continually present in his mind, and even in later years, which gave solidity to his group – the ideal of Cambridge, of young Cambridge, as the source from which the most vital movements in literature, art, and drama were to spring.

So Milton was duly honoured in the university of his youth. Mrs Brooke came over to see the performance, but as soon as she met Rupert afterwards, she realized he was utterly exhausted by his mental and physical efforts, and insisted on taking him home to Rugby to get over it. He protested weakly but he was so close to a collapse that he could not really argue.

Afer a few days' peace, he was able to write and apologize to his friends for having departed so suddenly. He could now take 'a little warm milk and Tennyson,' as he sat up in bed at School Field watching one of the late cricket matches in the fixture list, from the window of his room.

The muted thud of bat upon ball, echoed and emphasized by distant handclaps – sounds like these drifted to him as if straight from his past. Already Rugby seemed another age, though he had left it only two summers before. Now part of him belonged elsewhere, and he had grown away from it in growing up. Cambridge and his contemporaries meant more, now that the adolescent phase had really ended.

As soon as he was better, he said a temporary farewell to his parents again, waving to 'The Ranee' as he nicknamed his mother, and went down the town to the mock-Gothic railway station.

After this short rest, he was quite recovered, and found the university in the usual gaiety as end of term approached. A day or two before the Long Vac actually began, with the June weather warm and set, Brooke and Dalton suggested to a couple of others from King's that it would be nice to get out of the stifling rooms and sleep out of college in the field just over the river, beyond the Backs.

So under a full moon and brittle, brilliant midsummer stars, they took food and a blanket with them, pitched camp, and talked of eternity, girls and many other things. Then they settled down for an idyllic night, with the elusive sweet scents of summer all around, heightened by the night. The hours passed peacefully, but at first light one of the college porters espied them from quite a way off. They were breaking no regulations, but without troubling to investigate more closely, he scampered back to King's and reported to the Dean that three men and a woman were sleeping together in the Backs. Rupert wore his hair long, which accounted for the error! Things were soon sorted out, however, and no penalties imposed. The four of them walked back to breakfast still roaring over their 'orgy' of three men to one girl!

Just over a month later, came Rupert's twenty-first birthday, and about that week he was writing *Sleeping out: full moon*.

On 18 August, Brooke wrote from his home to Hugh Dalton, about to start on a walking holiday in Wales:

Your letter is admirably precise and leaves me utterly un-decided. I should love to sleep out with nothing but a few extra socks on. And yet . . . you in your low-lying Cambridge may not realise how cold it is o' nights – I don't know what to do. I shall do what the majority do. Tell me what the majority do.

If you and Ben are passing through this city on Wednesday, you'd better drop in and take lunch here, play tennis if you like, and take me on. The invitation holds good to all Fabians who pass through, Walesward, that day.

I don't know Mr. Service or his works. (Dalton had praised a Canadian poet in his letter). I don't think I should like them. I mistrust Sourdoughs. (The poems were called Songs of a Sourdough). What is a Sourdough? Pronounced Sour-dô or Sour-duff?

Human conversations are ever inconclusive. I told my mother that the chief end of Life was Pleasure, and she burst into tears. I await your Epiphany, your bright and glorious coming with many attendant daemons, to snatch me from my drab household. My uncle the Dean will be here. No matter. It will add to the Comedy. But Ben must not be blasphemous. I told the family a lot of people would be lunching here that day. 'Who and what kind?' they said. 'Oh! all right,' I vaguely smiled at them, 'practically Liberals. There's Dalton, son of a Canon, rather a Sourdo, you know – a Sourduff I mean. 'What's a Sourduff?' said my mother menacingly. 'A Colonial Sentimentalist,' I said, and drifted through Explanation for four meals. . .

The rumour about my age was quite true. I did it a fortnight ago. Leaving my unprofitable Youth and its fancies, I stepped across the Threshold of Manhood, jauntily, manfully; leaving a company of dancing children behind. I stumbled a little on the step which I did not perceive . . .'

Dalton himself could not come to Rugby on that occasion. They did meet a month later, however, when the famous Fabians, Sidney and Beatrice Webb, encountered some of the Cambridge University supporters at one of the Summer Schools. Among the group, too, were Marjery and Daphne Olivier, two of Brooke's favourite feminine companions. He was hardly yet aware of Noel as more than a girl.

In her diary for 15 September, 1908, Mrs Webb wrote:
'The Cambridge men are a remarkable set, fervent and brilliant.' She went on to describe Brooke as a 'poetic beauty,' though rightly judging Ben Keeling and Hugh Dalton as the two outstanding people politically. Mrs Webb ended another sentence in her memoir of Brooke on that first meeting: This was afterwards the famous Rupert Brooke who put me off the track by delivering a super-conceited lecture on the relation of the University man to the common herd of democracy. Perhaps she mistook Brooke's sincerity for snobbery.

Ben Keeling was certainly the leading light of the Cambridge Fabians, but the promise which Mrs Webb noticed had no chance of fulfilment, for Keeling was killed on the Somme in 1916.

During these open-air and Summer School holidays, Brooke and Dalton discovered the Belloc walking books, and Dalton observed how Belloc began to influence Brooke in rhythms, just as Christina Rossetti did in muted line endings.

The Long Vacation trailed into October, and Rupert spent a week or so in London, putting up at the National Liberal Club. From this address on the 7th he wrote:

> Dear Hugh,
> I stay here now,
> I meant to say—
> But you slid away—
> at that thing on Sunday
> This:
> Masterman is going to speak at Rugby and dine and sleep at our house . . . so come if you like. Rugby is hideous but you needn't notice it.
>
> Rupert

Masterman was still a favourite young Left leader, and Brooke was excited over the prospect of having him at School Field in the flesh!

Dalton was able to come this time, and the day went well. Brooke and Dalton saw Masterman safely off, and then Rupert suggested a look around the school. They made a tour of all the buildings and ended up in the School Chapel. Brooke pointed to the vacant space between the memorial tablets to Matthew Arnold and Clough. Half in fun, he said quietly:

'Look, they're keeping that place for me!'

Their chuckles echoed through the deserted chapel and continued across the grass to School Field. Now a tablet to Rupert Brooke in the chapel bears a profile of the poet over the complete text of his last sonnet, beginning:

If I should die, think only this of me:

Chapter Four

The Emerging Poet

The first book awaiting Brooke for review on his return to King's was *The Works of Tennyson* edited by Hallam, Lord Tennyson; ironic, in view of his recent references to warm milk and Tennyson. Somehow he could never become reconciled to the nineteenth-century romantic, and once wrote to St. John Lucas from Italy that 'the only things to read this benighted place supplies are Tennyson's poems and a London Directory of 1883. I've tried both and prefer the latter!' Tennyson made him feel as if he had consumed three basins of bread and milk with too much sugar in it. Altogether, Tennyson seemed doomed to be linked with milk in the mind of the passionate yet astringent Rupert Brooke.

Gradually, Brooke's work began to appear on a wider front than merely the *Cambridge Review*. More intriguing than his successes of this time, however, was the publication of the poem *Second Best* soon after it was written in the Mosker Books of Portland, Maine, two years prior to its English acceptance. No-one quite knows how this poem crossed the Atlantic, but probably Brooke sent it himself for, as a contemporary recalled, 'although Rupert's public form was the youthful poet, the real foundation of his character was a hard business faculty'. This should be taken to mean efficiency rather than real commercialism, which he hated.

The theme of *Second Best* is the eternal, one line in it urging:

Throw down your dreams of immortality.

This subject always concerned him, and he tended to doubt rather than disclaim completely, insisting instead that heaven is here on earth, and humanity should be what matters most. 'Our heaven is now, is won!'

Brooke loved to argue about it, and one night this term he was walking and talking with Dalton directly below Lowes Dickinson's rooms, on the top floor of Gibb's Building in the Front Court. Brooke was in the midst of making a passionate point and gesticulating emotionally when Dickinson's head, crowned with a white nightcap, popped out of the top window and called:

'I wish you'd go to bed. I can't sleep with all that chattering.'

Brooke and Dalton stopped suddenly in mid-debate, looked at each other through the gloom, and chuckled guiltily as they headed for their own rooms. Next morning, they went to apologize for disturbing Dickinson.

'What were you talking about, anyway?' he asked them.

'Immortality' they said in unison.

'Now if only I'd known that, I'd have come down and joined you.' This was one of Dickinson's favourite topics, too. Lowes Dickinson possessed a highly capable brain, and later when Brooke heard that he had been awarded the Kahn Travelling Fellowship to widen his mind, said:

'If they widen Goldie's mind any more, it'll break!' This was their nickname for Dickinson.

Brooke dashed down to London for a day or two during the Michaelmas Term and while at a Wagner concert in the Queen's Hall conducted by Henry Wood, his gaze strayed over to a gross man 'his heavy eyelids droop half-over'. Then Brooke mused on what the music meant to him, concluding that he:

> likes women in a crowded place.

The poem ended on a note of fleshy realism:

> his pendulous stomach hangs a-shaking.
> Thus was 'Wagner' born.

Christmas came round again, and as he had been working hard on his syllabus all term he felt the need of a complete change of scene

47

and occupation. Despite this need, it was with some doubts that he decided to join a party of young people bound for Switzerland and a holiday in the Alps. Here he relaxed utterly. He lived close to the crisp snows, touched by the sun into gold-glistening spectrum shades, sparkling crystal-clear as the air itself. He used skis and a toboggan, caught windy winter sunlight, and fell under the spell of the intoxicating, hypnotic heights – surrounding them and separating them from the rest of the real world. Or was that other world unreal, and this breathtaking beauty reality? It was difficult to decide. Hard enough to think at all, in the setting of such splendour.

The human scenery was not so bad, either, and he admitted that the girls in the group were better than they might have been. He was leading an almost unhealthily healthy life, eating enormously all the while.

And after days careering about on sleighs and toboggans, or slipping in the snow to joyous shrieks from the females, they all staggered, still weak from laughing, into the Swiss hotel for the evening meal and then singing and dancing. The Continental guests stared at each other in disbelief that these were the reserved Edwardian English.

'Est-ce possible? Les Anglais?'

A song and dance was not enough for Rupert.

'How about a play?' he suggested to them. An immediate chorus of confirmation greeted him. So they all got together to concoct a show to be presented at Christmas for the other guests staying there – whether they wanted it or not!

Rupert wrote an entire melodrama *From the Jaws of the Octopus* which was performed for the first and final time at Klosters. His part bore the impressive label of Eugene de Montmorency. Helen Verrall, one of the Cambridge girls whom he got to know better on the holiday, portrayed his creation of the Honourable Polly Technic, and among an assortment of extras were bobsleighers, skaters and private detectives.

The cast, in fact, outnumbered the onlookers of this epic, and everyone revelled in its climaxes. But, as always, the next day dawned, and they had to clamber aboard the Paris-bound train, looking coal-black against its background of snow and sun.

Mentally refreshed by all this nonsense, Brooke returned home to find that the two experimental choriambics he had written for the *Westminster Gazette* had won their prize and were published on 9 January 1909.

So to the Cambridge term once more and the Carbonari. The survival of such a casually formed group over two and a half years of developing life at a university was really remarkable, and testimony to the flexibility of its members. Early this term, on 5 February 1909, they assembled for their third annual dinner. The first one back in 1907 seemed far more than two years before. Now the entire strength turned out for the celebration in Rupert's rooms.

The sound of the water, lapping slightly to the night breeze, conveyed the familiar nautical air to the room, and even the light looked strangely like a hurricane lamp swaying in some cabin. Everyone was wonderfully bright; Rupert most of all. After the meal came the toasts – seven of them inscribed in a list on the menu card. And the very first, the loyal toast, turned out to be one of the shocks of the evening, for someone stood up and proposed it with a formula far from according to the programme. In fact, it turned out to be less than loyal, so perhaps the charcoal burners might have had some deep revolutionary purpose after all! Nigel Crompton looked down at his autographed menu card and read the rest of the toasts: 1) the King; 2) the Carbonari; 3) the World, the Flesh and the Devil; 4) our Better Selves; 5) Life; 6) Death; 7) the Great For-Ever. A different person proposed each one, until it came to the last, which Gerald Shove introduced. Then Rupert responded with a mellow, fluent, rambling chat, peppered with apt lines from poems. Ironic that it was he who spoke of For-Ever, as he always made it clear that he had to doubt its existence.

On nights like these, the Carbonari reached its zenith, all of them now more mature. Brooke read many papers to them, but perhaps his most memorable effort was a whole epic entitled *The Life and Death of John Rump, an English Gentleman.*

There was a prologue in heaven, when the soul of John Rump was launched for earth, and then followed the ironic story of his uneventful, unprofitable life. He became a master at a public school and helped to make another generation as useless as himself. Rump was a portrait of Rupert's father. In due time, Rump died, and the epilogue – like the prologue – was staged in heaven. Rupert was working himself up now to a frenzy of enthusiasm and he rounded it off with a superb and angry dialogue between John Rump and the Almighty. He alternated the voice with more and more difficulty as the argument heightened, but finally Rump won the day and Heaven vanished in a high wind.

'Bravo! That was terrific, Rupert' one of them called as he came to his last line and grinned. Dalton patted him on the back, too. The original paper is probably lost now, but Dalton always kept a copy of the death scene and the epilogue.

As winter passed, Brooke began to be drawn towards an outdoor life, Switzerland still lingered in his soul, and the seaside summer holidays. He took advantage of an early Easter to spend a short holiday in North Devon at Beckey Falls, where he indulged in chest expansion exercises and rambles over the hills as a combined attempt to develop his already presentable physique.

The house had a panorama ranging from the nearby grass and spring flowers of the garden, to the Falls, forest and hills, silhouetted on a skyline of pastels washed pale after the westerly winds and rain. Despite the mixed March weather, he relished this course of nature in which he also prescribed a vegetarian diet, few clothes, cold baths and hard work. His studies were for the classical tripos due to be taken in June. He was really working for it now and had set his mind on getting it if possible.

Brooke was beginning to look at himself and his life quite seriously now. But what were other people thinking of him? Someone in *The Meteor* thought that during this 1906–09 period he had sometimes been slightly cynical, intolerant and petulant, which are almost to be expected of a brilliant and admired undergraduate.

A better balance is given by Eddie Marsh, who found him 'self-examining and self-critical to the last degree, but hardly ever self-absorbed': by Frances Cornford: 'endlessly kind in helping me with my verses': by Mrs Asquith: 'he was noticing all the time . . . and he seemed never to forget the smallest detail': and by J. T. Sheppard: 'he was sensible enough and strong enough to take flattery, in the long run, for what it was worth; and he valued the affection that was critical, not flattering'.

The magic of May week assumed a special radiance in 1909, as it marked the meeting of Rupert Brooke and Henry James, 'as if patriarch greeted neophyte'. The two men met amid the glory of Cambridge when fashion, beauty, talent and manhood mingled with spring and summer at its most exquisite moment, transforming the shops and the streets, the colleges, meads and river into a week of wonderland out of the measure of time.

While some people maintained that Rupert always acted entirely unselfconsciously, others claimed that he was aware of the self-image he might be projecting for any given occasion. He was said to vary it according to the person and place. As Timothy Rogers reminds us about this initial meeting with Henry James, Rupert remarked: 'I did the fresh boyish stunt, and it was a great success!'

Henry James found Rupert 'a creature on whom the gods had smiled their brightest'. It was at King's, he recalled, 'during a short visit there in May week, or otherwise early in June 1909, I first, and as I was to find, very unforgettingly met him. He reappears to me as with his felicities all most promptly divinable, in that splendid setting of the river at the Backs; as to which indeed I remember vaguely wondering what it was left to such a place to do with the added, the verily wasted, grace of such a person, or how ever such a person could hold his own, as who should say, at such a pitch of simple scenic perfection.'

James became aware, too, of Brooke's 'irony, his liberty, his pleasantry, his paradox' for 'the medal of the mere pleasant has always a reverse for him'. This was completely true, confirmed by Brooke's own admission that intense surroundings or feelings often moved him to write in opposite vein. Although extremely emotional, he was never swamped by sentiment, but could spice it with another mood to give extra point and piquancy by contrast.

The last weeks approached before sitting the tripos, yet a steady stream of poems followed to the *Saturday Westminster*, which more often than otherwise won the prize in the contest set. Among these light offerings was 'a pretty lamentable ditty of love's flighte'.

To the *Basileon* for June 1909, Brooke contributed the sonnet *Day and Night*, while in the same magazine, that humorous yet pathetic man, Arthur Schloss, gave a vivid cameo of the Carbonari as they might relax after their many mental exertions among literature and the arts.

'Following the excellent example set by the Chetwynd Society, the Carbonari have also decided to give a ball.'

'It is beginning to be realised' said Mr Dalton in an interview with our representative, 'that the waltz and polka are an inadequate expression of the rhythmic emotions. We have arranged that our programme shall I contain several innovations. I myself shall cantilate "Whitman" while striking a three-stringed lyre and performing harmonic gyrations.'

'Other items of less importance will be as follows:-

Mr Reitlinger, a noted disciple of la Belle Duncan, will give a series of classical dances.

Mr Baker, his recorded prestissimo Jig for which he has been training since April.

Mr Shove will dance to the music of Gluck's newly discovered opera, "Le Roi aux Enfers."

Mr Ricard will croon folk songs to a minuet step, in sandals and a sombrero.

Mr Shand will sway to a "mouvement decadent" by Jules Hippolyte Montmartre (as discovered by the late Queen).

Finally Rupert Brooke will perform a dream-dance on tiptoe!'

The Carbonari had burned bright, never more so than now, but as June and the exams and the third year all ended, they decided to let it die. It had had a good life, Brooke thought, and they did not want to risk spoiling the memory by allowing it to live too long. In one way their last meeting marked a sad moment, but it also meant they had grown up since the autumn of '06, and recognized the need and inevitability of change in themselves and their lives. In any case, this particular evening was a perfect summer scene and the Carbonari would always stay in their memory, as an integral part of their years of youth.

Having taken this course, they broke up the last meeting early, with handshakes all round. Brooke wandered off among the stone buildings, serene and still in the gold-tints of sunset. The first star shone in a deepening blue sky, as he stopped by the Backs to look and listen. This was the magic moment of the day anywhere on earth, but at Cambridge, with its chimes and timelessness, it seemed touched into sheer unreality; the zenith, when one could burst with the beauty of it all.

Brooke let the day die all around him and settle into a

midsummer dusk, before he strolled back to his study, pushed the latticed window further open, and wrote the two words *Blue Evening* on a scrap of paper. When he went to bed at last, he had written the whole poem starting:

> The straight grey buildings, richly dimmer,
> The fiery windows, and the stream
> With willows leaning quietly over,
> The still ecstatic fading skies. . .

Here was a turning point, he knew, as the third year finished. The long vacation always conveyed the sense of coming change, anyway, and this time it was more so than ever.

Next day, Brooke quickened his walk to get to the notice board where the results of the classical tripos should be posted. This was silly, he told himself, hurrying like an eager schoolboy. But he had to know, and in a few minutes he did. He had failed a first, but there was the name safely among the second-class honours: R.C. Brooke. A moment of resentment, and then he shrugged his shoulders and went off in search of Dalton.

Already he and Hugh Dalton had decided that after three years of being confined in college, they had not been as brilliant as they ought, so were resolved to move out of King's the following term to detach themselves from the eddying currents of Cambridge which had apparently absorbed too much of their energies.

Dalton handed him a cup of coffee. Brooke thanked him, asking 'Where will you go, Hugh?'

Dalton considered as he stirred in his sugar.

'To Newnham, I think. And you?'

'I don't quite know yet, but I've the urge to try and find somewhere at Grantchester. It's just far enough out of town.'

'Well, I hope you do.'

After the coffee, Dalton finished his packing for the vacation, and some of the others came in to collect him for the train.

'I'll come along and see you all off' Rupert offered. Then, as the train wrenched itself out, leaving a fog of smoke scurrying along the platform, Brooke darted back to King's for lunch.

Another lovely day, and the rest of it to do as he liked. He thought over his idea of Grantchester and suddenly made up his mind to go there in the afternoon. He had an address of someone who might be able to put him up next term.

So as soon as lunch was over, he set out to stroll through the meadows to the village. Most people had left college already, and a silence hovered all around. He left the crenellated block of King's in the drowsy early afternoon. On the other side of the court, prickly pinnacles pointed into a haze-hot sky, and the figures on the clock shone bronze in the sun. Green grass with the sun on old stone, and the central arch framing a glimpse of the Backs, sloping slightly towards the water.

King's Parade led into Trumpington Street, then a turn right, to the narrows of Silver Street. He glanced down Queen's Lane for a last view of King's for an hour or two. Over the bridge, he walked up to the junction with Newnham Road, a reminder that his path and Dalton's were already parting a little. Brooke strolled past the row of tall, early-nineteenth century dwellings on the left, and smiled at the Malting House with its one oast alongside – one of the familiar landmarks on this road. Crossing to the meads, he saw the miniature falls of the river clogged with reeds. The river-side path followed the winding water, while poplars dotted the meadows with measured elegance. Branches bowed across the river, their tips almost meeting in the high-summer bloom. Chattering, fluttering crows sat dark against the sun in the treetops. Brooke breathed in deeply.

Back to the road for a few minutes, past a row of red villas, lately built, leading to Grantchester Meadows. Away on the left rose more regal poplars, and the Granta reached the meadows proper by a sharp bend, where two willows stirred the surface of the water.

Brooke looked straight ahead along the earthy path, and there, a mile off, nestled Grantchester church, trees clustering round its tower. Little inlets from the river wound to the edge of the foot-path, running 100 yards or so from the main stream. The sun glinted through laden boughs, as a flock of birds swept westward. His eyes followed them for a moment, till they veered out of sight. And over to the west, too, a row of tiny terraced houses heralded the beginnings of Grantchester on the road from Cambridge.

On the whim of the moment, he stopped, turned round, and walked backwards for a few yards, watching the spires of the city retreating. His shadow fell dark over the lush green grass, as the sun turned bonfire smoke to gold. The root of a nearby tree, jutting through the path, almost tripped him up, bringing him back to awareness again. He turned round to face the right way, and sauntered on across the meadows till the river ran away in the distance, and the path led to the heart of Grantchester opposite the church. His eye took him into its bounds, not for religious reasons, but for the sense of peace pervading it.

He had passed the church several times before, but not realized that its records went back to 1280, and the mid-fourteenth century chancel was decorated Gothic. The 56-foot tall tower came a little later at the end of that century. The western afternoon light brought the stained glass to life, with its portrayals of St Peter, St Andrew, St Paul, and at the back, Bede, Wycliffe and Tynedale. A shaft of sunlight, suffused dark red through one of the windows, fell at a familiar angle across the church, till it was broken by the back of one of the middle pews. Rupert walked around the interior, paused at the pulpit, and then moved back along the aisle. He found the atmosphere intensely restful, although he had little sympathy with the teachings of the church itself.

Out in the open again, he followed the road along to The Orchard, the house where he had heard there might be accommodation. Its sash windows and neat paintwork, with a white wash on all walls, appealed to him, and he sought out the lady in charge, a plump and weatherbeaten woman who succumbed inevitably to Rupert's radiant manner. He had soon arranged to stay there, and she showed him the room he would occupy, opening on to a creeper-covered veranda and looking over an old-English rose garden.

With that settled, he waved her a cheery farewell and continued his exploration. He thought of taking the path opposite the house to Barton and Haslingfield – the names sounded so intriguing – but decided instead to leave that for another day, and to go on towards the mill. Brooke passed the orchard that gave the house its name and blended into the meadow beyond, and the quiet little cottage of Yew Garth, home of Professor Cecil Warburton. At The Old Vicarage, he cast a casual look before proceeding to the pool below the mill.

There, in the midsummer mid-afternoon, he thought of the medieval church, and then of Chaucer in this very village, writing

The Miller of Trumpington. And his mind flowed on, like the water gurgling below the bridge, to the nineteenth century and Byron.

'Byron was a lodestar to Brooke' Bertrand Russell said to me. And strangely, Byron was at Cambridge and Grantchester exactly a century before Brooke. He had been born ninety-nine years earlier than Rupert and, like him, died among the legendary Greek islands.

Brooke sat on a stone wall and gazed into the pool. What a wonderful day. Here was history, poetry, and the essence of England at her best; here at the heart of culture in Cambridge. This was an afternoon to be remembered, when he first met Grantchester on intimate terms. What Rugby had been until 1906, and King's till 1909, Grantchester was to become for the next three or four years and as a symbol for the rest of his life. He sensed it first on this day by the mill.

There was no point in delay, so after a return to Rugby to see his home, he moved his things into The Orchard. Then he had scarcely settled there when he left it for August and most of September, first to re-join his parents at a house in Clevedon on the Bristol Channel.

With their agreement, Rupert issued invitations to most of his friends to come down there during the summer. Eddie Marsh was one who accepted, though their friendship was yet to develop.

Rupert had been seeing Noel Olivier on and off for two or three years now, and Mrs Brooke was beginning to believe he felt seriously about the girl, who was still quite young. When he went to his mother to tell her whom he wanted to invite to Clevedon, she said:

'Yes, you can invite the Oliviers, if you want to, Rupert, but not that young one!' Despite this, he continued to see Noel, either at the Oliviers' home in Limpsfield, Surrey, or at holiday parties or elsewhere. Later on, Rupert asked Noel to marry him and at some stage he also proposed to Bryn, one of her three older sisters!

Dalton was one of the party, too, who accepted the Somerset invitation. While he and a few others were down with Rupert, they decided one day to write and invite Ramsay Macdonald to Clevedon with them. The letter was dispatched within the hour, but although they knew he was at his home, he never answered their joint invitation. Dalton gave him a bad mark for this, but no-one really missed him.

After Clevedon, Brooke and Dalton joined four other Fabians at the Summer School in North Wales for a few days, where the Webbs were presiding. It was still summer, and spirits ran as high as the temperature. At one stage, a member of the group was found by the Webbs locked outside on a ground-floor balcony of the house, in company with a chamber pot! The Webbs were not at all amused at this horseplay, which they felt both unedifying and immature. When the luckless person was finally let indoors, the whole younger set collapsed on their beds to the accompaniment of various comments pertaining to the vessel!

Mrs Webb found the talks they all had interesting, but thought that they did not want to learn. She concluded that the egotism of the young university men was colossal and wondered if they were worth bothering about. She had failed to appreciate that it was a vacation, the summer one, too, and these men were still pretty young. Brooke and Dalton, for all their wit and wisdom, only celebrated their respective twenty-second birthdays a week or two earlier.

While these rags were going on in Wales, the September number of the *English Review* appeared with four of Brooke's poems, including *Blue Evening* and *Finding*.

Norman Douglas was on the staff of this periodical in 1909 and during the earlier part of the vacation met Brooke three or four times at the office. Douglas liked his work more than most which they received for consideration, but did not fall under the Brooke personal spell so much as many others. Indeed, Douglas felt, rightly or not, that if the two of them were ever left stranded on a desert island, sooner or later they would come to the end of their conversational tether. For Douglas admitted that he liked someone he could dislike or with whom he could quarrel! There was no disliking Brooke, he felt, nor was quarrelling possible with a supremely contented man.

Douglas did not regard his poetry of that time as outstanding, but would describe it as possessing a breezy obviousness. Brooke was a dear, transparent, social creature. But he had a spine, was vertebrate. Douglas saw the Brooke of summer 1909 as a man with a positive gift of yea-saying to life: assimilative, zestful, unafraid of realities.

The editor of the *English Review*, incidentally, Austin Harrison, revealed several instances of indecision about accepting poetry submitted by some of Brooke's contemporaries, and Rupert himself. One unfortunate contributor actually died while waiting for Harrison to make up his mind about a poem. And one of James Elroy Flecker's best poems – either *The Golden Journey to Samarkand* or *Gates of Damascus* – reposed for a long time before being finally rejected. Flecker was consumptive and poor, so a small cheque could have helped him a lot.

But *Blue Evening* and the three others by Brooke were accepted. And the vacation ended. Then a day or two after the start of term, he ran into Dalton in Cambridge. Both of them were now out of college, Brooke at Grantchester, shedding its russet leaves, and Dalton reading economics at Newnham.

Just as they met, some of the year's freshmen floundered past them into King's.

'Don't these young men make you feel old?' Dalton asked Rupert in mock earnest.

'No' he said, 'not old, only tremendous!'

They had come quite a way since that first Sunday when they met on the steps of the provost's lodge three years ago – two fellow freshmen.

Chapter Five

To Grantchester and The Old Vicarage

'My dear chap,' Rupert greeted an old friend in the university, 'I did not really begin to live till I went out of college. You can picture me leading the rustic life, broken by occasional visits to Cambridge; keeping poultry and a cow; playing simple tunes on a pan pipe; bathing every evening at sunset; and taking all my meals in a rose garden!' This should all be taken with some salt, to allow for Brooke's naturally extravagant expression, but it was still clear that here was a way of living he liked.

His verse, too began to develop at the same time. It has been said by H.W. Garrod that Brooke began to be a great poet when he got away from Cambridge. Garrod accounts for some half a dozen worthwhile poems of the Cambridge period ending in the summer of 1909, and these only written by running away from the people who admired him, by getting clear of Cambridge. Except for this number, nothing he wrote inside college equals almost anything outside. It is amazing how little Brooke was spoilt considering how much he was fêted by his contemporaries. His character could so easily have been ruined.

Meanwhile, although his verse matured, it was not at the expense of other activities he considered really important. From The Orchard that autumn he wrote to a Miss Garrett in Girton, about a meeting with the Webbs, in a hasty handwriting:-

I am enclosing a notice of the Webb meeting on Thursday. If there's any place in Girton where such a thing may be posted, can you put it up? As you see, it's not an exclusively Fabian thing, and other people may like to go. If any dons or elderly people that you hear of, who are interested in Poor Law Reform, want to go, I will send you reserved seats for them if you let me know how many. There will only be a few rows reserved: and only for such people.

Yours sincerely
Rupert Brooke

It may be very full.

Brooke's illuminating personal letters were multiplied by many more such official notes as these. Sybil Pye recalls that in one of their discussions the phrase 'an artistic eye in a business head' caught Brooke's attention; he said he believed the combination was possible, and he certainly aimed at making it so. She was sure he had a happy talent for organization.

This immediate post-graduate era was when Arthur Benson, master of Magdalene College, knew Brooke best: never intimately, but quite well. Here is his recollection:

My impression of him is vivid and clear, which is hardly to be wondered at, for he was very unlike other people. His charm, his enjoyment of life, his great personal beauty, the imperishable quality of some of his poems, and the strange suddenness of his death have combined to create a sort of legend about him, and to invest him with a mysterious sanctity which would both have amazed and amused him – and vexed him. For he has become not a very animated and actual human being, but a figure like Linus or Hylas or Lycidas, solemnised by the shadows of his untimely death. Yet the very existence of this legend, with its enfolding rarity, is of itself abundant testimony to the high and abiding quality of his charm and his work.

An enthusiastic undergraduate talked to me about him with generous and overwhelming enthusiasm, and indeed had made it his business to collect Rupert's fugitive verses. Later he brought me a packet of these to see. I own I did not think them greatly promising – conventional in their deliberate modernity, uneven, and bizarre.

Then I met him in the rooms of another undergrad. He strolled in very late. He was far more striking than exactly handsome in outline. His eyes were small and deeply set, his features healthily rounded, his lips frank and expressive. It was the colouring of face and hair which gave a special character. The hair rose very thickly from his forehead, and fell in rather stiff, arched locks on either side – he grew it full and overlong. It was a beautiful dark auburn tint inclining to red, with an underlying golden gleam in it.

His complexion was richly coloured and his face much tanned, with the tinge of a sun-ripened fruit. He was strongly built, but inclined to be sturdy and even clumsy, rather than graceful and lithe. His feet and hands were somewhat large, and set rather stiffly on their joints. His hands had no expressiveness or grace. Nor did he sit or move with any suppleness, but lounged or rather huddled in his chair . . . his glance and regard were frank and friendly.

He was thought to have a real critical gift and considerable erudition. But he was impatient of college restraint and lived often at Grantchester, working, bathing and exploring the country on foot or with a bicycle.

He came to dinner with us. I don't remember his saying anything markedly memorable, but just joined in the talk in a lively and companionable way. When he went away, we agreed that he was not in the smallest degree spoilt by all the attention and adoration he received, but was living a tough, enthusiastic life with strong preferences, and without any pose. He had no touch of intensiveness, of affectation. After this I came to know him better. One day he came dressed in a coal-black flannel shirt with a bright red tie and a suit of grey homespun.

The Michaelmas term passed, with Brooke working hard for the Charles Oldham Shakespeare Prize, which he won in December. Christmas came round again and another party was being organized for Switzerland, which he joined with more readiness than last time.

Brooke could recapture every emotion from ecstasy to despair, and the rough crossing to France on a late December day inspired another of his intense, 'objectionable' pieces, *A Channel Passage* which ended with this tongue-in-cheek rhyme:

And still the sick ship rolls. 'Tis hard, I tell ye,
To choose 'twixt love and nausea, heart and belly.

Earlier reference to brown gobbets and sobs and slobber were judged offensive by some select circles: even Eddie Marsh found them unnecessarily unpleasant.

Rupert travelled with old friends – Dudley Ward, Jacques Raverat, and Daphne and Marjery Olivier. But not Noel. Helen Verrall came, too, and she assisted him with what threatened to become an annual event for the other visitors to the hotel: the dramatic offering.

'Let's have something musical this year' Rupert suggested. 'I know, how about a comic opera?'

Helen beamed at this brainwave. Brooke at once set about composing a libretto, fitting light verses to existing music such as the *Soldiers' Chorus* from Faust.

'It's going to be called *The Super-Ski*' he announced next day with mock importance, 'and we'll all have to wear ski-suits. And another thing. I can't sing, so someone will have to provide a voice from the wings while I mime my part.' Dudley and Jacques both offered to do this, and eventually all the characters were allotted.

After a few evenings' rehearsal, New Year's Day was chosen as a fitting day for the final performance, which went with a fine swing from first chorus to last. But the reception from the foreign guests was, as previously, one of tolerant indifference deteriorating towards actual aggression as the essentially English humour of Rupert's lyrics was lost on them.

The next morning, the faded lounge still showed evidence of *The Super-Ski* even after they had all left on the first stage of their journey home. Brooke accompanied them, but was suffering from minor poisoning through bad water. He did not say much about it, as they stopped for several days at Basle and Paris to view paintings and other sights, yet all the time he was staggering round with a temperature, feeling miserably ill. Luckily, the Channel crossing was calmer, and at last he got back to Rugby after what seemed endless days of trailing around Europe.

At once he sank into bed, still with a temperature, but his own illness paled before the news awaiting him at home: his father had just had a minor stroke and was being taken to London to consult a specialist. The trip proved futile, for the doctor could neither comfort nor treat him much. Back at School Field, Rupert was recovering from flu which followed his poisoning, but realized he could not leave his mother at the moment until things changed. Although not selfish by nature, he was appreciating how much more Grantchester meant to him than Rugby.

Following his practice of writing in opposite vein to any intense prevailing mood, he passed a convalescent day on 11 January composing a light love-piece looking back at *The One before the Last*.

> how faded dreams of Nineteen-ten
> were Hell in Nineteen-five.

This he followed with two sonnets more in the mood of the cloud-filled sky behind the empty school buildings opposite.

Rupert had not long to wait for a change in the situation. A few days later, his father suffered a second stroke and died, just as Rupert was putting an arm round his mother to comfort her. School Field suddenly seemed cold and even more empty. No voices of juniors broke its chilly passages, and rain drooped down the window panes. Despite John Rump and all he had thought of his father, Rupert felt an intense sense of tragedy, similar to the days following his brother's death.

To add to it all, Mr Brooke was buried on the same day that the boys trooped back to School Field from their Christmas holidays. The news buzzed round in a moment, of course, and small groups of boys stood huddled in various parts of the house or garden throughout the day. Rupert helped his mother survive the funeral, but the shock had been severe to her. And then he went down again with a further bout of influenza. He lived through a concentrated few days of depression, but because of their intensity and his unquenchable verve, he bounced back to life determined to save his mother having to move house, at least temporarily.

'I'm all right now, mother, and I've had an idea. I'm going to take over as housemaster tomorrow. I'll see the head and try to arrange it at once.'

The head agreed readily to this measure, and so Rupert stayed the entire Easter term of ten weeks as acting housemaster at School Field. In a week or two, he recovered his spirits completely, and was surprised to discover himself a good master with a bluff Christian tone that was wholly pedagogic, as he put it to a friend. He received respect, too, as the seniors still remembered him from their 05–06 days and how he represented the school 'at various violent games'. And he in his turn genuinely liked the fifty-three boys under his care, although he could not bear to think that they would inevitably follow the well-worn convention to Cambridge, and ultimately take their unimaginative place in the upper classes of the country. This was what made teaching at public school intolerable for him: the system of snobbery which moulded most of them into the reverse of individuality. His Fabian feelings reached their strongest this year.

Cambridge was all right as long as you were aware of its dangers, and kept clear of that fatal mould of mediocrity. Meanwhile, what he would be missing there this term came home to him when he contributed an article on *Richard II* to the *Cambridge Review*, preceding a performance to be given by the Marlowe Society. He was sick to miss this, he told Frances Cornford. But by compensation, he gained a sense of self-reliance through his term at Rugby. It widened his sphere of experience still more. Across these three months, incidentally, he had been writing *Dust* which he completed at the same time as his locum was over, too.

In April Brooke bade a final goodbye to School Field, as he helped his mother move into a small, uninteresting house in Bilton Road, Rugby, with only a number to mark it from other identical dwellings on each flank. The term had been stimulating in one way, but now he realized afresh the significance of his father's death – he would never see School Field again. From now on, it was Bilton Road. Even the name seemed to reflect its lack of individuality. How could you get out of the rut of routine in a road like that?

With Mrs Brooke safely installed, she insisted that he took an Easter holiday, his first relaxation from strain since that operatic evening on New Year's Night.

Once more at Lulworth, he tramped across the Downs and breathed the south-west spring wind, which smoothed the short grass in its path. South, nothing but sun and sea; north, cottages nestling in the Dorset dales. Everywhere, the rugged, ragged grandeur of Purbeck stone homes, and in the distance, the outline of Corfe Castle.

Here he forgot that henceforth there would be no tennis court at home, that he had no father, and had lost one brother. Before lunch, he read Elizabethan plays at the rate of twenty a week, and then in the afternoons he clambered up the cliffs to sort them all out in his mind. Three a day was quite an average to assimilate. This work on the Elizabethans went towards the Harness Prize Essay. In one provocative mood, he declared with the exaggeration known so well to his friends that the only good plays written between 1500 and 1650 were *The Faithful Shepherdess* and perhaps *Antony and Cleopatra*! The mood of the moment, was sincerely felt, but not to be taken too seriously as lasting dramatic criticism. His essay won the prize later in the year, under the title *Puritanism as represented or referred to in the early English drama up to 1642.*

Probably at Lulworth, too, he wrote one of the best of his sonnets, *The Hill*, notable among other things for a poignantly perceptive last line:

And then you suddenly cried, and turned away.

Lulworth was doing Brooke a lot of good. One day during the Rugby term, he had gone to see Arthur Benson at Cambridge and talked with occasional animation, interspersed with moods of depression.

'My mind has become stuffy and unreliable,' he told Benson; 'I feel I want to meet strangers, and get a current of new thoughts and images.' Lulworth was the first step in this direction.

Back at Cambridge, the two men dined together again and Benson noticed that Brooke seemed infinitely better, even more handsome and charming. They talked discursively about books, and Brooke laughed at his host's humorous tales, conveying to Benson nothing of the typical intellectual. He was easily pleased in life, Benson thought, and observed how Rupert preferred the talk to wander where it would.

At the end of April, with Grantchester garlanded in early apple blossom, Brooke went back there for the first time that year. He said he wanted to see the spring coming to the village, and arrived at its height. What was the idyllic influence the place offered? A timeless tranquillity?

Grantchester had a shy, evasive beauty; an unmistakable though not exceptional charm. Rupert discovered it more and more as the weeks went by.

Behind the church stood an old manor house comfortably embedded in trees; and there the road turned at a sharp angle by a mossy wall of mouldering brick, and followed the line of the fosse of the Roman camp which gives its name to the place. On the left, a little lower down, The Old Vicarage, a house of ancient red brick and a big garden behind it, fringed by great chestnut trees, ran down to the river. Here, in a straggling wilderness, was a rockery of ecclesiastical fragments, and a ruinous old building of clunch and tiles, designed as a garden-house but with an excrescence like an apse which gave it the air of having been intended, in a rococo manner, to present the appearance of a chapel or oratory.

Pursuing the main road, which zigzags with extraordinary pertinacity, Brooke used to pass a pleasant, tiled, orange-plastered house in an ample garden, which cheered him invariably with its warm Mediterranean colouring. The road came out by Grantchester Mill, passing between the mill and the pool.

This was not the mill made famous by Chaucer's tale – the ruins of that stood farther up the stream – but a modern structure whose actual mill kept grumbling and groaning while the stream spun and gurgled into the deep pool; floating off among green meadows and under high, dark-shadowing chestnuts into a wide and glimmering reach of water.

Rupert found that the mill-leat embraced a broad islet, deep in meadow grass on either side of the road and all enclosed by towering elms, the wilderness of Trumpington Hall, and the dark shadowy groves that brood over Byron's Pool.

Arthur Benson loved this spot, too, recording that 'in a day of high summer you could hardly find a sweeter place; all embowered in branching trees and close-set orchard; the fowls picking up the fallen grain; the lazy anglers by the stream; the deep-brimmed pool with the breaking bubbles and the darting fish; the fragrant, fresh, weedy scent, and the distant clink of rowlocks over the grass. A dreaming charm. . .

The gracious Granta winding through the woods; wistaria-clad houses on a lowly hillock; blossom moving magically in a spring sunset – these are the things which cannot change.

Grantchester had peace, too. There was just one cab, to be hired for weddings or funerals, driven by a coachman whose top hat was a tempting target for stones in summer, or winter snowballs. Dick Cox, the village carrier, smoked his pipe while his pony lolled along at leisure.

Then there were the village simpletons. Alf was lame and cross-eyed, yet walked to Cambridge each day to take up his post as crossing sweeper along the road by the Backs. His crony was called Spider Riddle, for his tall, spindly appearance. These two often quarrelled, to the gentle amusement of the villagers. They would shout abuse at one another and aim wild blows through the air – but both were afraid to come close enough to risk being hit! Then the deep peace returned to Grantchester.

Brooke moved enchanted through this reverie of 'apple blossom and the river and sunsets' but still managed more or less daily touch with Cambridge. He was elected president of the Fabians and in a room of Gibbs' Buildings at the south-west corner of the front court, they would all foregather for socialism, beer, bread and cheese. Another activity later this summer was to be a repetition of *Faustus*, while yet a further group enlivened by the twin spirits of Brooke and Dalton was the Fish and Chimney, where plays of all periods were read and discussed.

In fact, Brooke found himself busier than ever, cycling to and from Cambridge, or entertaining his host of friends out at The Orchard. Several of the university people actually lived at Grantchester, too, including the sisters Sybil and Margaret Pye, who often walked down the road from their own home to visit Brooke at the guest house.

One evening while Rupert was reading poetry to them and some others, the scents of spring pervading the room coupled with Brooke's mellifluous delivery, prompted Margaret to make a delightfully spontaneous sketch of him as he spoke. On the back of the paper she drew another, more fanciful, impression of him supposedly drinking Dudley Ward's health in the latter's rooms at St John's College.

The Pye girls became close friends of Brooke during this year and next. As the days stretched longer and longer, they talked to him of everything under the summer sun, and Sybil made mental memories of each golden day. Rupert had this capacity with everyone – of making them feel that the place and the time were both special, that this was a moment for which they had been born.

Sybil loved talking to him, for she had never known so sympathetic a conversational opponent. He had a way of working her opinion into his reply so that his dissension seemed merely a comment on some conclusion already reached; the result of his natural kindness and innate sense of good manners.

At other times, he would sit in silence among a group, looking from speaker to speaker till they thought he had wandered far from their present themes; but a quick comment or question, with a sudden intentness in his look, showed a mind awake and aware.

Occasionally his abstraction did go deeper. A group of them, including the Pye girls, were in the middle of a favourite game of the day, Up Jenkins, in which someone had to try and point out a sixpence hidden beneath one of the other's hands. It came to Rupert's turn to order all hands to be laid palm downwards on the table. Then, instead of proceeding to guess which one concealed the coin, he just sat looking distantly at them till good-natured shouts of impatience echoed down the line of players. Suddenly, smiling in half-apology, he jerked himself to consciousness and explained: 'Oh, but hands are so beautiful!'

Brooke was normally much more practically aware than this, though, and had a strong capacity for organizing not only business but social affairs as well. One day during the May Week of 1910, three separate parties fell on the same day, and as everyone was anxious not to refuse any one of them, the three festivities were combined to meet in the Pye's garden.

There was clearly a danger here, for among the mutual acquaintances a number were naturally strange to each other, and to the tastes and outlook of the rest. In fact, the task of trying to merge such diverse elements into anything approaching a sympathetic social entity seemed so hard as to be not worth attempting but Rupert thought otherwise and in fact, he did automatically, by his very presence, merely moving from group to group dissolving their incongruities and creating links. The contrast of his conspicuously attractive appearance and his unobtrusive manner stamped the scene with an atmosphere hardly any of them forgot. His sincere interest in everything was quickly catching, so that lively conversation soon superseded the conventional commonplaces which had threatened to dampen the entire affair. Brooke knew them all, and liked them all. That was his unconscious outlook on life.

With June joyfully launched by the celebrations of May Week, Brooke took every advantage of the summer. On most days, he swept up an armful of books into a canoe moored behind The Orchard, and just let it drift along, with only his left hand dangling a paddle through the water. As the boat glided beneath the branches, seen again in the glass-still stream, he made rapid, jerky notes from books on any scraps of paper available, and whether alone or accompanied he read out random passages to enjoy the sound of the forms and cadences. Spenser, Ben Jonson, Beaumont, Fletcher and Webster all seemed to receive an added grace when heard here, among the dark reflected trees and the sudden wide openings across the flat, heat-misty meadows.

Often he paused at one particular open space. The proportions of the trees that bound it, and the pale far-running distance between, made it seem to him a happy setting for a play he would write. Here Rupert sat, superbly suspended, among serene depth and shadowed height.

He came to know each curve of the course the river took, each tree-clump that marked it, with an uncanny intimacy. Sometimes he brought the Pye girls home by river from Cambridge after an evening event there, and coming up with him in a canoe those three miles to Grantchester on a dark starless night, this intimacy became startling. Every possible landmark seemed merged in a blanket of black, and even the water-surface ceased to show the faintest gleam, meeting its muffled banks invisibly and unheard. Except for the soft splash of the paddles, they might have been floating in some totally new medium, free of boundaries, out of all reach, in a fourth dimension.

But Brooke kept on course. He knew, he told Sybil and Margaret, when they were nearing home by the sound of a certain poplar that grew there – for its leaves rustled faintly even on nights like this.

The girls peered at each other, then out into the dark, and only half-believed him; so many poplars rose by that river, and it sounded absurd of Rupert to be able to recognize one. Yet he was right. At a certain point, there was the slightest sound of leaves stirring on the suggestion of a breeze. Rupert shipped his paddle for a second to hear.

'Listen! There it is – can you hear?'

And sure enough, he landed them without hesitation at Grantchester by their own garden, mooring the canoe as easily as if it were midday.

On another afternoon, he picked them up, and they tied the canoe to a tree trunk while they sat on the river bank. Rupert started to give the British poets marks according to his view of their worth. He was enjoying himself tremendously, but when it came to awarding Wordsworth only a low rating, Sybil Pye protested, maintaining that he had written the most beautiful two-stanza poem in the language.

'That's a very sweeping statement' he replied, 'can you support it?'

Sybil quoted in full:

A slumber did my spirit seal . . .

When she reached the end, she looked up at him, still expecting to be challenged. But instead, the whole air had altered; he sat silent and absorbed, the serious critic replacing his previous extravagance. This change in Rupert Brooke was as sudden and gracious as his other transitions, of movement and voice.

But Brooke was human; it would be wrong to depict him otherwise. One teatime at The Orchard, two sisters were with him. The elder was supposed to be his current love, but another visitor there noticed that he was spending quite a lot of the time flirting with the younger girl, and enjoyed their combined efforts to attract him. He was constantly searching for fresh excitement, expression, interest, so too much should not be made of this: they were just part of the infinitely varied and vivid personality.

On 1 June 1910, *Day that I have loved* appeared in the *Westminster Gazette*. During June, he reported Will Crook's lecture to the Fabians in the university *Review*, and in the first week of July went home to attend a Fabian conference. Sidney Webb was one of the speakers and in Rupert's words to Dalton 'old Shaw popped up and down'.

But the climax of the academic year came after the term was finished. A party of fifty German students were expected early in August at Cambridge, and in their honour the Marlowe Society decided to repeat *Faustus*.

Before rehearsals for this began, however, the Pye girls, with Rupert and one or two others, sat in a garden where wild briar stocks hung laced together in festoons under the darkly grouped trees. And here one evening at midsummer they read *Antony and Cleopatra* with Rupert playing Antony. When he came to the great climax and, with a voice scarcely audible, read the soliloquy starting:

> I will o'ertake thee, Cleopatra, and
> Weep for my pardon, so it must be, for now
> All length is torture. . .

the very tree shapes seemed to take on a tragic significance in the summer dusk. Few of them were ever able to read those lines again without hearing his voice.

Brooke's quotable familiarity with Shakespeare was quite extraordinary; the sonnets seemed all there in his head, and lovely lines from them and the plays would be dropped into the air at all sorts of casual moments, and always with such feeling for their true qualities that they remained transfixed in the mind, with the background of place and theme which had prompted them.

Faustus rehearsals were held in the Pye's house at Grantchester during the second half of July. Then when the work was over, Rupert would read to the Pye girls, the Cornfords, and the rest of the company in the sitting room. It was a small and low room, not unlike Rupert's study at King's, with a lamp slung from the ceiling and a narrow door opening straight into the dusk-dark garden. On quiet nights, when watery scents and sounds drifted up from the river, the room almost suggested the cabin of a ship. Brooke sat with his book at a table just below the lamp, the door and the dark sky immediately behind him. The lamplight outlined the proportions of forehead, cheek, chin.

He was entirely English, but when he spoke, and especially as now when he read aloud, the clearness of his diction and the expressive freedom in the movement of his lips suggested races whose speech is quicker than ours, and whose use of consonants more adroit and telling. It would actually have been quite possible to lip-read what he was narrating.

Poems of periods from John Donne onwards he read to them. Short stanzas by Donne and Swinburne, Synge's *Deirdre* and Meredith's *Modern Love* made the most impact, the Meredith sonnet-cycle giving him scope for that unforced inflection and variety which so characterized his voice. He would drop from an airy lightness to a sombre, deep emotion with a suddenness and grace that made them catch their breath with wonder.

In spite of this quality of voice and rare power of employing it, he still had no particular talent for acting, so was relegated to the role of Chorus for *Faustus*. Even in this minor part, there was missing at the actual performance in August all the charm of those garden rehearsals, complete with his expressive gestures. With a podgy bull-terrier as the only audience, Rupert stood barefooted under a briar-arch, and appealed with passion to the dog and any chance observer – giving them the joy that the audience would miss.

One day he lay on the floor of the Pye's sitting room playing with another dog, a puppy, who seemed, as he said, able to turn right round inside his skin. The same rapid elasticity marked both their movements, the darting dog and the hands which showed such quick, flexible precision. They were strong and expressive, these hands, with a thumb well divided from the palm. Their shape and articulation imparted a Blake-like quality to his freely direct gestures at rehearsal. And to one onlooker at least, they provoked a strange experience. For when Nijinski danced *The Rose* in London for the first time soon afterwards, this friend had the queer feeling of having seen it somewhere before – until the resemblance turned out to be Rupert practising his gestures for the Chorus in *Faustus*.

When friends thought of Rupert, they saw his characteristic pose, full-length on the ground and supported on one or both elbows. He was sure to adopt this sooner or later, either on the grass or the floor. An alternative was to tuck his knees under his chin and clasp his hands around his calves for support. But the full-length posture was favourite, and somehow seemed to be equally suitable for reading, writing, or talking – or all three at once!

Once a strange female was introduced to him at an inopportune moment while he lay on the floor. He had no time to change his position, so made a gravely courteous salutation – an actual bow from the floor, which looked like the height of elegance. The inescapable truth was that Brooke could never appear less than captivating.

Him, I count him, well-starred.

Matthew Arnold might have written this of his poet successor from Rugby.

So the night of *Faustus* came, and as the curtain fell, the real exuberance erupted. Term was finished, and *Faustus* too. Cambridge leapt gaily and weirdly to life under a fitful harvest moon, as the entire company, still in their costumes of devils, ecclesiastics, virtues and vices, hired a charabanc and drove in procession through the sleepy streets to the Cornfords' home in Madingley Road. Helen of Troy, deserted and desolate at missing the bus, managed to find a bicycle and sped passionately after the troupe, who leaned out of the conveyance cheering her on!

Safely at Conduit Head, the Cornfords' home, they danced and drank by the light of torches and a bonfire. Rupert had been wearing the long-and-full black gown of Chorus, cut like a medieval scholar's cloak, with a cap the same sombre colour. These were deemed quite hopeless for dancing, so they had all searched through the stage props till they found him a close-fitting purple doublet, dashing to a degree, and long hose in similar style. A many-pointed gold crown was set on his head, and he was ready for the fray.

Outside the ring of lights, the night had drawn as dark as the doublet, and his figure melted into it. Then the spurting gleam from the bonfire would light the points of the crown, conveying to his head a ghostly detachment! The lights also caught the golden tone of his hair, escaped by now from the clutches of the crown and flapping freely as the dance grew wilder. And amid all the bacchanalia, those blazing-bright, intense, merry eyes in a face absorbed yet aware, alert to capture elusive experience.

Beer and cider and sandwiches kept them going long past midnight, and the oasis of light flared for a mile or more over the townscape. Finally, exhausted, they grabbed up the lowering torches and formed a return procession on foot down the Madingley Road.

The middle of an August night came before everyone reached their beds. A maze of emotion twisted through Rupert's brain as he lay, slightly cider-drunk, recalling eight hectic hours since six that evening. He had kissed one of the girls deliriously in the Cornfords' garden. Now the night was over. They were all dispersed. The torches died down. The moment was past. The kiss was gone. There had been others. There would be more. What did it all mean?

The rest of August, Rupert spent with Dudley Ward touring towns on the south coast by caravan to promote the Minority Report on the Poor Law. At the end of their route, they reached a prearranged camping spot on the far side of the New Forest, beside the remote Beaulieu River. Here they met friends again, and slept in tents close to the coast, west of the Solent.

Unlike the previous years at Cliveden, Somerset, Noel Olivier was at Beaulieu. She and Rupert lived idyllic days there, walking, embracing, under the green cover of branches overhead. They talked of plans for the future. Yet their love did not last. Summer in Hampshire turned to autumn in Cambridge.

Brooke returned to Rugby for a day or two before starting the fresh term, and there he finished *The Life Beyond*, a sonnet on a lost love. It is dated from April to September, and ends with the haunting lines:

> I thought when love for you died, I should die.
> It's dead. Alone, most strangely, I live on.

Chapter Six

Back to Cambridge for the final Year

For his fifth and final year, Brooke returned to Cambridge. The Michaelmas term was still a day or two off, but he wanted to see how the new Fabian rooms were progressing.

His early period of Youthful Tragedy, as he dubbed it, had passed into perspective and an innate optimism asserted itself most of the time now, or anti-pessimism, as he called it. Just before leaving Rugby for Cambridge this time, he wrote a long letter to Ben Keeling, mainstay of the Cambridge Fabians, explaining his present attitude to life. The nearest word he could coin was mysticism – not meaning that the whole world was good, but rather an absence of despair that it was not. A subtle difference! In fact, he saw so much beauty and sudden significance in everyday things that they made his breath stop 'with a gulp of certainty and happiness'.

Hugh Dalton had left last term, and began to see much less of Brooke. They had had many memorable times together, which neither ever forgot; the wrench of ending the close friendship was less severe than it might have been, because it was spread over twelve months. Now it had finally happened, it appeared – like other things in Brooke's life – to fall into some sort of perspective. The inevitability of change. Now he almost welcomed change for its own sake, yet still the hankering remained after the old faces and friends.

The only Fabian older than Rupert now, he dismissed as positively senile, so he felt paternal and almost ancient himself among the current group. They were less cramped in the newly acquired rooms, than in Rupert's own, and it was in these fresh surroundings on 24 November 1910, that he read them his lecture on 'Democracy and the Art'. Dashed off spontaneously in pencil at some speed, it was brusque and colloquial, with none of his literary grace, yet still extremely effective in its arguments for endowing artists from public funds.

In art as in other fields, Brooke's 'Beardsley etchings' period was another phase of the past now, for he had moved over to Rodin, El Greco and Augustus John. In literature, his taste and critical faculties were more mature than ever, and at the end of 1910, reviewing two volumes of *The Cambridge History of English Literature*, he was merciless in his condemnation of its style:

> Dreariness, vagueness and dull dull discomfort settle down on the reader. It is like trying to smell flowers through a blanket. It is amazing that experts and professors of English Literature familiar with so many alive and glowing styles, should write such uniform lustreless English, with all the faults of journalese – the flaccidity, the circumlocutions, the trite lifeless unmeaning metaphors, the interminable substantives without its occasional brightness.

The week before Christmas and the end of the year he spent at Lulworth with the Raverats, where he wrote a light *Sonnet Reversed* on New Year's Day, 1911, while Jacques sketched him idly and dated the drawing – 1.1.11.

A momentous date Rupert agreed, 'the start of the Georgian era.'

From Lulworth, Brooke began a long Continental tour, starting at Munich where Dr Dent had given him numerous introductions. He stayed for three months here, looked after at the pension by a fat Frau Ewald. He liked the Germans but found their culture oppressive and to be resisted at all costs. As the *Meteor* recorded subsequently at Rugby, he said: 'I have sampled and sought out German culture. It has changed all my views. I am wildly in favour of 19 new Dreadnoughts! German culture must never prevail.'

Despite this outburst, he would sit here in Munich on most nights after a visit to the opera or other diversion, reading the latest *Times* and sipping glasses of hot milk! One evening when he was trying to unfold the massive format of the Literary Supplement, his elbow caught the glass and he knocked the milk all over himself. It was the signal for the entire content of customers in the café to fuss around him, mopping with cloths and dabbing and drying him!

Rupert sat in the opera and let the swirling sounds of Wagner engulf his senses. Then when he had heard enough brass chords, he decided to risk *Rosenkavalier* and Richard Strauss. And into the nights, he talked to charming people like a Mr Leuba, so lovingly different from what an unsuccessful journalist would be like in England. But he missed most of the brilliance of conversation in the Cambridge manner, arguments with the Raverats, Cornfords, Justin Brooke and Katherine Cox. He visualized Francis and Frances Cornford; one smoking, the other sitting in her favourite chair on the right of the fire at Conduit Head. And as he sat sipping his milk, Conduit Head automatically reminded him of that night after *Faustus* the previous August. The cider, the torches, the girl in the garden. England, England. All these blurred images blended into a single searing yearning. He longed for England, yet wrote poetry which was improving every month. *Dead Men's Love* he dated 27 February and *The Fish* the following month. The latter was intended as a lyric, but he turned it into its present seventy-six line form.

Rupert walked home to the pension in a spring sunset. A German girl was singing folk-songs, accompanying herself on the lute as she sat by a casement window. The jolly Frau Ewald licked her brush as she painted a portrait, one of a regular flow of pictures which the woman produced; she believed in quantity if not imperishable quality. Her son, Paul, called to Rupert in greeting, to chat about his own days at Cambridge. Of the rest, most were English people with clerical background – not quite in tune with Rupert.

He had enjoyed himself in Munich, but finally decided it was time to quit the clatter of the German city, where he vowed he ate and slept too much. So he went on to Florence, which he had not seen since his Rugby days.

Here he joined his godfather, Robert Whitelaw, and fell once more under the magic mood of Fiesole, its cypresses and spring sun. Originally he had had visions of journeying to Turkey and the mystic Middle East, but this was far enough after all. For even as he felt the fresh Italian heat beating down on him through the clear

April air, he was thinking of Grantchester again – and now of The Old Vicarage where he would be staying from May onwards.

Rupert followed the spring back north across Europe, and found its end in the garden at Grantchester. Already he knew the house from previous visits, and was attached to it from the day he moved in there.

Where did the magic for Brooke lie in this house? Less with its looks than its character, in a sensitive setting of garden, trees, meadows and stream. The building itself was a wide place on two main storeys and dormer windows to the attic in the roof above them. Aged brown tiles, ivy groping over mellow rust bricks, and a steep gable on the west side, all added to its air of antiquity. Inside was a wonder of decrepitude: an elderly stuffed tiger stood fierce guard in black and tan at the top of the stairs, while rooms opened off from one another in an intriguing, inviting way.

Rupert liked immensely the yellow-glass door to an elaborately wrought veranda, as it gave the garden a sunny tinge on the dullest day, when seen from inside. The scene from the veranda itself was rambling; sweet-smelling shrubs and foliage, with here and there, some relics of the house's eighteenth-century associations, such as a sundial sticking out from the dried-up basin of the round pond.

Once-formal flower beds ran wild with neglect, and rambler roses twisted unkempt into sweetly strangled arbours. Lichen clothed the outside of the veranda, and even that baroque summer house at the far right end of the garden was dilapidated. Yet despite it all, The Old Vicarage was a living place, and Brooke much preferred its natural environment to a vapidly formal garden. Once within the picket fence, he felt, a world of past peace breathed gently to life. The afternoon sun shone, throwing shade from the elms on the right further across the lawn, till the old sundial in the centre stood all but engulfed. Not that it would have mattered; time counted for little here.

By now, Rupert was learning to love going in the water, as well as on it, and he spent hours at various reaches of the river. On Sunday mornings especially, one of his friends used to wake him early to bathe in the dam above Byron's Pool. Time after time on those slumbrous Sunday mornings, with the first haze hardly off the meadows, he would try to dive, but he invariably failed, hitting the water absolutely flat! Although this must have hurt him, he seemed to love it. Afterwards, they would trot back for breakfast, often in the garden of The Old Vicarage, tucking into a meal of eggs followed by bread and butter and honey.

Brooke's bedroom in the Vicarage was permanently littered with books – English, French, and German – in wild disorder. After breakfast, they might go up there to browse through his collection. And in spring, summer, and even autumn, he always dressed in the same way, with an open cricket shirt, flannels and no socks. This garb was at that time regarded as eccentric but Brooke did not care at all, claiming that he could dress on three pounds a year! If the weather was really favourable, he discarded shoes as well as socks to reveal his set of prehensile toes, known to be able to pick up a variety of objects and perform feats arousing envy among his admirers.

He was virtually a vegetarian all the time at Grantchester, for he could not eat creatures with whom he felt a kinship. Fish were not included in this category, but even so, some of his friends wondered whether he was having enough sustenance for his heavy mental and physical exertions.

This sympathy for living creatures kept him busy in the garden, where young frogs abounded, the grass being as damp as it was glowing green. Their lives, alleged Rupert, were extremely perilous, for the landlord ate them in secret! So Brooke's long form often appeared at the oddest hours of the day and evening squatting in the long grass, guiding them out of the open and into safer, sheltered paths.

Now that the Grantchester period had really got under way, he was shaving more rarely – and badly! Mentally, however, he kept as meticulous as ever and always ready to attack a careless thinker. Despite this, Brooke tolerated fools well – even bad poets who must be among the worst of fools. The last impression that Brooke's bathing companion had of him was lunching in London together, when Rupert wore a blue shirt with a red tie and drank stout readily.

That same summer of 1911, Helen Houlton, a daughter of the local schoolmaster, often went to visit a friend of hers, Kitty Bentley, who was living at The Old Vicarage. Helen and her sister, Dorothy, stole through the sleeping village very early in the mornings to bathe, throwing small stones up to Kitty's window to awaken her. They called out softly, so as not to disturb the other guests, but often Brooke appeared at his window and waved gaily to them. Or if he had been up earlier, they met him as he came back from a dip while they were making their way down to the river from the garden.

The girls learned to swim here, where the water was only waist deep, and then when they could manage more safely, they found deeper reaches. They chose early morning or late evening for bathing, because no-one was about, and their mother feared they might shock the local folk! The female form had to be kept religiously hidden. Even their long, voluminous and unbecoming swimming costumes were considered daring.

The two girls ran barefoot through the dew-drop meadows, collected Kitty, and then hurried down to the water. Several years later they felt that Brooke must have meant them – Dorothy, Kitty and Helen – as they read:

> And when the day is young and sweet,
>   Gild gloriously the bare feet
>   That run to bathe . . .
>   And there the shadowed waters fresh
>   Lean up to embrace the naked flesh.

They hoped he never saw them in that state, although it was possible. For later on, when they bathed by moonlight in the friendly Granta, they tired of their cumbersome costumes, threw them on the bank with wild shrieks, and swam along the dark, deserted river – feeling wicked but free! And Brooke wrote:

> They bathe by day, they bathe by night

Virginia Woolf got to know Rupert well that summer of 1911 and stayed at Grantchester. Together they swam quite naked, to their mutual delight at the unconventionality. Virginia spent a week at Grantchester and remembered Rupert as 'consciously and defiantly pagan'. She thought him 'kind and interesting, substantial and good-hearted' but she 'didn't think then much of his poetry, which he read aloud on the lawn'. Virginia and Rupert exchanged letters later on. And still later she felt that his best work was still to come. . .

Rupert, the Pye girls, and one or two others used to bathe by the moon above Byron's Pool. One glorious night, after the exhilaration of swimming in the silver sheen of the river, he clambered up a young poplar to dry himself.

'Be careful, Rupert' one of them warned from below.

'I'm all right thanks – it's wonderful up here.'

And at that precise second, they all heard his loud unembarrassed laugh as the branch bent right over double under his weight – and he was left hanging the wrong way up, with his long hair brushing the grass. In the moonlight they could see his face convulsed with glee at this unaccustomed view of the world.

On the way home that night, he told them that he intended to rent a small but useful boathouse near The Old Vicarage. So true enough, he sought out the owner and arranged the deal. But as Rupert investigated it further, he found it looked very drear, so he decided to decorate the inner walls with a collection of dashing drawings of nudes. No-one would mind, surely? At least he wasn't painting them outside. What could be pleasanter or more artistic? For several days he spent hours at the job, and the result revealed him as a talented figure artist. If he had not been absorbed with metre, it might have been murals, obviously.

Throughout that summer, the boathouse and its decor served its purpose well, and his art attracted comment from all the Cambridge circle who saw it. But when he finally relinquished the lease to a set of church people, the first thing they did was to have those uninhibited, sinful sketches whitewashed into oblivion where they belonged!

To another friend of the times, he told: come prepared for bathing and clad in primitive clothes. The order of each day, he added, was to talk eight hours, read eight hours, and sleep eight. Actually, exercise took up several hours, not only swimming, but walking and cycling. One morning while he was working on a difficult poem, he plodded on till one o'clock and then ran almost all the way to Haslingfield and back before a belated lunch, thinking what should come next. His tall outline diminished to a tiny silhouette jogging along against a frosty sun. The bicycle, of course, was coming into its own, and still new enough to intrigue Brooke. He

81

used it as a useful way of getting to the university on the increasingly rare days necessary.

Practically every day, Brooke was seen somewhere around Grantchester, mainly in the meadows. One evening in late June, the Houlton girls were dawdling homewards when they saw him standing quite still near a tall clump of elms, on a little hill called Tartar's Well. He was gazing straight into the sunset, his head thrown high and fair hair wisping in the wind. Now Tartar's Well has vanished from the local landscape, but that image of Brooke endures.

Sometime during that same summer, Virginia Woolf and Ka Cox joined Rupert and others at the camp of Clifford Bridge beside the River Teign in south Devon. When the two girls got there, the rest of the party had gone out for the day, 'Leaving nothing for Ka Cox and Virginia to eat on their arrival save a rotting blackberry pudding'. (Quentin Bell on Virginia Woolf). But the weather was fine and they enjoyed good music and good conversation around the nightly camp fire. Rupert's circle of friends rippled on outwards. Another companion of the 1911 era was David Garnett, who visited him at Grantchester during the summer term. Then when holiday time came around again, Garnett and Brooke joined a week's sailing trip on the Norfolk Broads, a change from Somerset and Dorset.

This time all the Olivier girls came, and one or two other young people completed the party – with the inevitable chaperone in the form of Dr Rogers! In those days, the Broads were practically deserted. A single sail provided the power for their wherry, and when the wind was contrary or dropped altogether, they lowered this canvas quite professionally and a patient horse appeared, attached to a tow rope and complete with a boy sitting sideways on its back.

Life on the Broads was free and peaceful. They swam in the mornings, with Rupert still trying to master the craft of diving. Then they lay on deck and talked, as the boat slid smoothly through the East Anglian water. Rupert sat forward, propped against the mast, re-writing his thesis on John Webster and the Elizabethan Drama, which had occupied him on and off for most of the year – including his time in Germany, where he had done very little research, but written a number of poems. Unfortunately, at that time Garnett had not read any Elizabethan dramatist except Shakespeare, so when Rupert read some extracts to him, they did not mean very much.

They had a sailing dinghy in tow, and if the breeze tempted them, a few went off to sail. Then came the long, golden evenings, when the wherry was moored by the bank and the couple of paid hands who navigated it departed to a pub.

The days ended with a swim in the darkness and a night-scented kiss on deck. Then with the girls' goodnights ringing in their ears, Brooke and Garnett returned to the cabin they shared. For Garnett, this was the week of his closest friendship with Brooke, whose immense charm and intelligence he thought were completely unspoilt. In their midnight talks, Brooke was simple, sincere and intimate, with a certain lazy warmth. The water lapped at the side of the boat and all was well with their world: the new Georgian world of 1911.

Chapter Seven

Just now the lilac is in bloom . . .

Brooke's poetry of this period could hardly have been less like that by Frances Cornford, who believed – according to Rupert – that poetry should be short, simple, naive. Yet despite their different styles, they were good friends and candid critics of each other's work.

For some months now, they had nursed hopes of bringing out volumes of their poems, but so far nothing had materialized. Brooke told her how the reviewers would mistake their respective sexes, as so often happened, and say that Mr Cornford had some pretty thoughts, but Miss Brooke was always intolerable! Or else they could be called Major Cornford and the Widow Brooke.

Now, in September 1911, Brooke finally found a publisher who was interested in handling a volume of his verse. The man with the vision to encourage Brooke was the late Frank Sidgwick, of Sidgwick and Jackson, who had also been at Rugby. He had read random poems by Brooke in one or two of the literary periodicals, when Brooke brought him the first collection of poems. So Sidgwick already knew, before reading the complete manuscript, that Brooke could write with extreme beauty, and could run with a savage joy to the other end of the gamut.

At this initial meeting with Rupert Brooke, Sidgwick was surprised and pleased to discern that he had none of the ordinary illusions of young poets. The publisher accepted the volume in principle, but asked to see Brooke again to discuss exactly which poems should appear. At this next meeting, Brooke told Sidgwick that he was eager not to overbalance the book in the direction of unimportant prettiness, and so defended the inclusion of certain poems which Sidgwick queried on the grounds of suitability.

'Well', Brooke persevered, 'people need not read the parts which are new and serious, or they think objectionable. You know, I occasionally feel, like Ophelia, that I've turned "thought and affliction, passion, hell itself . . . to favour and to prettiness".'

Sidgwick respected his wishes and risked the inclusion of some 'unpleasant' or 'provocative' poems. One of Brooke's continual struggles was to avoid the mere prettiness in poetry and aim higher and deeper. It was an immense effort for him to achieve the satisfactory expression, he told Sidgwick.

Into the 'immeasurably autumnal' air pervading Grantchester, Brooke continued his consciously pagan existence. His feet still bare, his bed often in the open, disdaining tobacco and meat; a complicated compound of vigour and sensitivity. But however 'sunburnt and slapdash' – as a contemporary described him and his literature – they were both intensely, vitally alive.

He worked hard at his poetry all the time. Proofs of his book fluttered on leaf-strewn grass, while unfinished poems lay about all over the place, with his habit of leaving spaces in an unfinished phrase or line. One day during 1911, for instance, he was completing *Town and Country* when he reached the penultimate verse. Squatting in the garden at Grantchester, he asked his friends who were there what was the highest thing in nature. Then he glanced around, decided it was a leaf in the sun, and completed the first two lines of that verse, which had borne a blank space till then:

Unconscious and unpassionate and still,
Cloud-like we lean and stare as bright leaves stare

To his friends he continued to be just Rupert Brooke; that was enough. They still did not think of him primarily as a poet.

That first volume of poems was typeset and printed in the sedate Victorian building of Billings, just outside Guildford railway station, and even the compositors expressed excitement in some of its lines as they handled the type and pulled proofs of it – certainly an unusual occurrence.

And meanwhile, up at Grantchester, at the same time as passing the proofs, he was 'wallowing in Webster'. But as the autumn wore on, he was finding it increasingly essential to be near the British Museum to gather the final facts for his thesis. Yet however hospitable Eddie Marsh invariably was, he felt he could not stay there for a long period, so for the next six or seven weeks, he found some dreary rooms in Charlotte Street, Bloomsbury, their only advantage being the proximity to the British Museum.

Here he suffered from the sudden contrast between his healthy Grantchester life and the late autumn mists of the metropolis. He worked far too hard all day on Webster, without troubling much about food, and afterwards he went round to Marsh's flat in Gray's Inn, or to other friends in the artistic area. Several times he tottered across the lawns of Gray's Inn, barely able to reach the gaunt, deep-buff building. This pace could not be kept up for long, it was clear. Always he had that tendency towards sickness – apparent after using up too much nervous energy – although he had not been really ill yet.

London life became too much for him by the middle of November, so as soon as he had got his material from the Museum, he told Marsh he would not stay any longer but would write the final draft back at Grantchester. This had to be finished by Christmas, and actually took the latter half of November and earlier part of December, when The Old Vicarage was a 'House of Usher' matching his mood of gloom and fatigue.

How strange, he thought, the dramatic difference between summer and winter at the same place: from sun and splendour to dank despair. He looked out past the veranda, but saw only a stark tracery of trees, black-branched, their lives in suspense; the grass no longer grew; the river looked muddy, morose; and a grey fog-shroud settled over it all. He was worn out.

Near the end of this time, his younger brother visited Grantchester and found that Rupert had hardly been to bed for a week, trying to complete his thesis.

'You must ease up, Rupert, you know, or you'll have a break-down. No blessed thesis is worth that.'

Rupert nodded, but was compelled to go on till he had finished it. As he scrawled the last line, he sank back in a chair exhausted and lay there for several hours. But he was too tired to rest, he had gone too far. He felt he must get away from it all again, so packed a case quickly and delivered the thesis to Cambridge. Then he

1. Rupert Brooke, 1913.

2. Rupert Brooke in the Cricket XI, Rugby 1906.

3. Dudley Ward at the end, Geoffrey Keynes looking down the table and Ethel Pye in the foreground.

4. The Orchard, 1910. Rupert Brooke facing Sybil Pye.

5. Rupert Brooke and Dudley Ward on the river at Grantchester.

6. Rupert at a picnic.

7. *Left to right:* Noel Olivier, Maitland Radford, Virginia Stephen (Woolf), Rupert Brooke

8. Noel Olivier in camp with one of the Pye sisters.

9. At work in the garden of The Old Vicarage, Grantchester, 1910.

10. Rupert Brooke
    with Brynhild
    Olivier in the
    New Forest.

11. Cathleen
    Nesbitt with
    a seagull.

12. Rupert Brooke with Duncan Campbell Scott in Canada, 1913.

13. Rupert Brooke reading aloud to Helena Cornford and friend at Cley-next-the-Sea, Norfolk, 2 August 1914, just before the outbreak of war.

14. Lieutenant Rupert Brooke, Royal Naval Division, 1914.

15. Rupert Brooke's grave on the island of Scyros in the Aegean.

caught the late train on to London to see Marsh again. Gradually restlessness was growing within him which could not be satisfied, stifled; an urge to be elsewhere, and then a nostalgia for where he had been. An eternal buffeting between past and present, here and there. In London, he soon realized how ill he was and hurried home to the sanctuary of Bilton Road a week before Christmas.

By now, *Poems, 1911* were published, although he was past caring about their reception, for at the best of times he lost interest in anything as soon as he had created it. He could not claim complete indifference, however, for he had fought hard for the retention of those 'objectionable' poems.

Lust was one of those he succeeded in keeping, although he compromised – in a letter dated 20 September – on a modified title of *Libido*. Despite this, Brooke regretted his weakness, for whenever he came across a copy of the book, he struck out *Libido* with a definite, defiant line and wrote *Lust* in large capitals instead! In the copy he inscribed for Francis and Frances Cornford, later acquired by the collector John Schroder, this alteration has been made, and Brooke has also changed 'greasy' to 'queasy' in the poem *Jealousy*.

The line now reads:

Senility's queasy furtive love-making,

The reviews reached Brooke at Rugby and on the whole could be called most encouraging, although the half-dozen allegedly unpleasant poems received critical comment and attention out of all proportion to their quantity in the total of fifty.

The Spectator applauded the poems wholeheartedly, commenting that 'unlike most youthful work, it shows a curious absence of imitation and a strenuous originality . . . a book of rare and remarkable promise.'

The Saturday Review, remarking rather obscurely, told him to 'mar no more trees with writing love-songs in their bark'. Edward Thomas, in the *Daily Chronicle*, forecast that Brooke would be a poet and not a little one going on in exhortation: 'Copies should be bought by every one over forty who has never been under forty. It will be a revelation.'

Finally, among the daily papers, *The Times*, too, foresaw a future for him: 'Here is clearly a rich nature – sensuous, eager, brave – fighting eagerly towards the truth. And already Mr Brooke can show now and then an almost uncanny achievement.'

Quite a few exceptions were taken to the 'unpleasant' poems, which were too realistic for 1911, one reviewer calling it 'a volume of blague'. And public feeling, like that of Rupert's friends, could be summed up in Arthur Benson's view of the poems, 'some very charming, some strangely ugly'. But the notice which meant the most to Brooke was by Eddie Marsh in the *Poetry Review*: 'A too conscientious critic might argue that he is not sincere, that he rides round the world as though it were a circus, crashing through the emotions as if through paper hoops . . . Meanwhile let us be thankful for a man who can make so much beauty.'

Although Brooke still felt very tired over Christmas, he was determined to keep an arrangement, made a long time before, to meet Cambridge friends at a fortnight's reading party down in Lulworth, starting from the last few days of the year.

He managed to get there, but almost on arrival had the nervous collapse which had been threatening since the autumn. The final cause of the collapse was Ka Cox. Rupert felt close to both Noel Olivier and Ka, but this episode at Lulworth seems to have precipitated stronger feelings for Ka. She and Lytton Strachey formed two of the reading party, while the painter Henry Lamb arrived two or three days later. Lamb started flirting with Ka, much to Rupert's fury. He became even more livid when she told him that she felt attracted to Lamb – the upshot being Rupert's near breakdown. All he could do was to stay in bed, with hardly any food or sleep, until he could get back to his doctor who saw at once that he had lost a lot of weight and diagnosed 'a seriously introspective condition'. 'You need an utter change from all this' the doctor decided. 'Your mother is staying in Cannes, so I advise you to go over and join her there. Just the thing for you at present.'

Rupert acquiesced, and made his weary way to the South of France, where the stuffy, upper-class atmosphere immediately grated on him. He was determined to leave as soon as he could decently do so, and making his excuses to the completely uncomprehending Mrs Brooke, he went on to the more congenial and familiar pension at Munich.

The cure here for his previous lack of food and sleep seemed to be overeating and oversleeping, coupled with complete absence of exercise and thought. Brooke really had to force himself into this state of mental stagnation so alien to his normal nature. It was a real effort to relax.

A letter from Eddie Marsh, then on Admiralty duties in Portsmouth, cheered him early in February, for it enclosed the notice of his poems, which Marsh was proposing for *Poetry Review*. Marsh mentioned how *Dead Men's Love* offended many people. Brooke could never understand these objections.

Hands out, they hurried, knee to knee

– this was the type of line which purported to repel pre-war readers, still not free from starchy Victorian hypocrisy.

Rupert rose late at the pension, lived off milk and stout – separately – and generally did as he was told by the capable, capacious Frau Ewald. And between her successful efforts to restore his health, she painted a portrait of Brooke, which for a while hung on one of the walls in the common room at King's. It reflected rather a sick man still, and could not be considered a work of art.

The secret and surprising thing was that, unknown to Mrs Brooke, Rupert and Ka had arranged to meet on the Continent. They went on to Munich from a Verona rendezvous. Ka looked after him as a lover and, as he gained strength, she broke it to him that she had still been meeting Henry Lamb. Rupert felt appalled that Ka could divide her feelings in this way. Towards the end of February they returned home. Rupert wrote nothing at that time, except his letters.

Despite this dramatic phase in their relationship, Rupert remained close to Ka. But by the time he managed to reverse her feelings the following year, he no longer really loved her. The irony of life. . . Yet when he left half a dozen letters written in case of his death, the one to Ka ended: 'You were the best thing I found in life. If I have memory, I shall remember. You know what I want for you. I hope you will be happy, marry and have children. It is a good thing I die. Good-bye child. Rupert.'

This constant inconstancy of hearts worried him sometimes.

There did not seem to be sense in it. He wanted love to last always, but it never did. So he drifted from one girl to another. Searching for something. Through the years, this is what his life became, a search, an endless quest – for what? Brooke did not know, could not tell. Life, love, their power, their meaning, their lack of meaning.

So he went on searching. Judging by a letter to Katherine in March 1912, soon after he got back to England, they still seemed to be on good terms. After a walk in springtime Sussex trying to trace the home of Henry James, he and a friend reached Rye.

Here, Rupert sat down in the medieval Mermaid Club and wrote to her lightheartedly, recounting their adventures across the middle of Sussex. When he had finished, he strolled out in the afternoon air of the old town. The teashops with the little Tudor windows were starting to serve; the church stood reminding him of the one at Grantchester; and at four o'clock stillness descended on the timbered facades of that little world within a world which has been Rye for four centuries or more. Nothing stirred, though a new-fangled motor car struck an incongruous note. Rupert lingered in Rye for a day or two, remembering Ka. This was a place of love: the rooftops of Rye, set high on a hill. And because he had loved Ka, he wrote flippantly. That familiar opposite vein reacting against his feelings.

Meanwhile in March or April, he wrote two poems, each reflecting in the season of spring, the emotions of fading love. The haunting *Beauty and Beauty* with its misty ecstasies 'eddying, dizzying, closing round'.

And then in its second stanza:

> Where Beauty and Beauty met,
> Earth's still a-tremble there,
> And winds are scented yet.
> And memory-soft the air,
> Bosoming, folding glints of light,
> And shreds of shadowy laughter;
> Not the tears that fill the years
> After – after –

And after, came the *Song* with its sadness of that spring:

90

All suddenly the wind comes soft,
And spring is here again;
And the hawthorn quickens with buds of green,
And my heart with buds of pain.

One or two recent writers have placed undue emphasis on a single homosexual encounter between Brooke and a friend while under the stresses of Cambridge. Rupert himself described this in a characteristicaly natural letter soon afterwards. Perhaps it would be more accurate to ascribe any neurosis he might have suffered to the fact that English girls did not normally consummate a love affair at that period: perhaps inhibiting to someone as intense as Rupert. Certainly homosexuality as a way of life repelled him and, as Timothy Rogers has pointed out, Rupert 'cut Lytton Strachey dead, in public, in the foyer at Drury Lane'.

Eddie Marsh went up to Rugby to stay for a few days with Rupert, who had added a bout of 'flu to the nervous illness. There they walked along the Avon's banks, as Brooke did when a boy. He felt better after this, and cheered up still more with the arrival of Geoffrey Keynes for an evening meal.

Gradually Rupert was recovering. At Easter, he was advised to have another change of scene, so went down to Lyndhurst, where he stayed at a house called Beach Shade, a name he was quick to see symbolized his current state of mind. For here in the heart of the ancient New Forest, he wrote to Hugh Dalton of his troubles and his travels:

Dear Hugh,
    You were good to me. It doesn't matter about the scientist who got a fellowship for two reasons
    (1) Nothing matters.
    (2) They will give me a fellowship next year. The electors seem agreed on that.
    The scientist, you see, had no more shots. I have one more. Both our dissertations were extremely good. He discovered a very important thing about the Blood of Coal Miners. It needs far less oxygen than you think. And, it follows, they can live for longer and far oftener when the Worst happens, than you suppose.

91

Friend of my laughing, careless youth, where are those golden hours now? Where now the shrill mirth of our burgeoning intellects? And by what dubious and deleterious ways am I come down to this place of shadows and eyeless pain? In truth, I have been for some months in Hell. I have been very ill. I am very ill. In all probability I shall be very ill. It is thought by those that know me best (viz. myself) that I shall die. Nor do I greatly want to live, the savour of life having oddly left it, and my mind being worn and flabby, a tenth of anything it used to be.

I do nothing. I eat and sleep and rest. My thoughts buzz drearily in a vacuum. I went in January to a slightly American nerve-specialist who said I was deplorably unwell. He made me drink stout and swallow the compressed blood of bullocks. In consequence I am now enormously fat. Boys laugh at me in the street. But that is partly, also, in account of my manner. For I am more than a little gone in my head, since my collapse.

I go back to Germany soon. They are a slow race and will not know I am stupid. I shall never appear in England again. I shall never write poetry or limpid prose again. I may ultimately become a sub-reader of English Philology in the Johns Hopkins University, Wa. (or Ma. or Ra . . .).

I am a despicable, toothless creature and I mock at the Spring.

I salute you from these depths. Give my love to the Middle Temple.

Ever
Rupert.

Lulworth, Cannes, Munich, Lyndhurst, with its New Forest memories of Noel. And now back to Germany again. This time, however, he went for a return visit to Berlin, where he spent most of the time with Dudley Ward and his wife.

The spring had really reached England by the mellow and magic early days of May. But over in Berlin, Brooke sat at a table of the Café des Westens. He looked around him at the sweating Germans, and then up at the humid, cloud-strewn sky. A throbbing wave of loneliness, longing, clutched him – and he scrawled down:

Just now the lilac is in bloom,
All before my little room;

No more need be said. The clatter of the café faded from his ears; the smell of sweat changed magically to poppy and pansy; his ears saw beyond the gilt furniture and the urgent city, away to the sights of springtime in Grantchester – cool, clean and clear – and the sense-swirling, intoxicating, simple splendour of it. He ached for England with a sincere, searing pain. And the only way to stop it was to convey his emotions. In a few days, he had completed 140 lines of 'this hurried stuff' as he called it when sending it on to Eddie Marsh.

Here, for the first time, he perfected that mature marriage of light and lyric; wit and wonder. *The Old Vicarage, Grantchester* has come to be recognized as one of the most memorably evocative landscapes in all literature. No-one reading it has failed to be transported deep into the greenery of Grantchester at that supreme moment of spring.

As Mary Sturgeon has said, 'a satirical imp darts into a line and out again . . . one catches half a dozen incidental impressions which pique the mind with contrasting effects and yet contribute to the prevailing sense of intolerable desire for home'.

The poem did not have to wait long for publication. Only a month after Marsh had received it and realized its worth, it appeared in the June 1912 *Basileon* under the title of 'Fragments from a poem to be entitled *The Sentimental Exile*'.The original version included the phrase 'Polizei not verboten' instead of the revised 'Where das Betreten's not verboten.'

Before leaving Berlin in the sticky summer heat, he worked for a month on a one-act play which turned out to be the melodrama *Lithuania*, his only work for the stage.

The play is based on the idea of a son, long since left home, returning with a fortune to his poor peasant family, who kill him for the money before discovering who he is. John Drinkwater acknowledged that though homespun, almost threadbare, in texture, it was not without beauty that none but a poet could have achieved. Incidentally, it was during this summer that Drinkwater first met Brooke on an important day.

Rupert returned from Berlin in June, happier, heavier and

healthier. One day in September, it occurred to Marsh and Brooke that there should be scope for a book of collected poems by a dozen or so of the younger poets, an idea which before long blossomed into the anthology of Georgian Poetry, 1911–12. Marsh gathered some prospective contributors along to hear of this proposal, and then they all went along to visit the home-to-be of the *Poetry Review* at 35 Devonshire Street, Bloomsbury.

That first occasion when Drinkwater met Brooke, there were only a few moments they could talk together, yet even there he got the impression of an extraordinarily alert intelligence, finely equipped with both wit and penetrative power. Drinkwater realized that no-one of Brooke's years could ever have had in greater measure the gifts that could be used to make easily swayed admiration gape: and no man was ever more wholly indifferent to any such conquests. Drinkwater found humour in abundance, but of witty insincerity, no trace. Never was a personality more finely balanced. He was properly glad of his qualities; also, he was properly careless of them.

This meeting between Brooke and Drinkwater was on 20 September, when they lunched at Marsh's home in Raymond Buildings by Gray's Inn. Among the other guests were Wilfred Gibson, Harold Munro, and Arundel de Re, associate editor of *Poetry Review*. It was also Brooke's first meeting with Gibson. After the exciting seeds were sown for the Georgian Poetry book, the day ended with Marsh's putting up for the night, Rupert, Gibson, and their musician friend, Denis Browne.

Eddie Marsh was performing his self-imposed task of patronage well, although there were some who remained convinced that beneath all his efforts lay a certain snobbery and an inclination for reflected glory. Whatever the truth, Rupert did meet several of his brighter contemporaries through the medium of Marsh: Walter de la Mare, John Masefield, John Galsworthy and the legendary figures of Katherine Mansfield and John Middleton Murry.

Brooke accepted an invitation to visit Katherine and John at their home in the country. Rupert Brooke, the debonair, Murry called him. Brooke told them, with a wry laugh, macabre and horrifying tales of old women in lovely houses being devoured by their own cats, and of strange and sinister happenings among the Lithuanian peasants. This was the play, of course.

One early autumn evening, Brooke, Frederick Goodyear, Katherine Mansfield and Murry tramped miles over the salt marshes in the dusk from Runcton Cottage, singing the choruses of Goodyear's innumerable songs. A queer quartet vanishing into the gloom as their voices wafted away into the night. Then after the rustic interlude which Rupert relished, he returned to the life of London and Georgian Poetry.

Chapter Eight

Georgian Poetry and
Travels to Europe

Exactly three weeks after the luncheon launching the first book of Georgian Poetry, Eddie Marsh had gathered and prepared enough examples of the major young poets to compose a representative volume, and on the next day he actually sent them to the printer to be set. In just over two months, the book appeared. But before this, Rupert went to stay with the Wards in Berlin again, from where during November he sent frequent communications concerning techniques for marketing the book successfully.

From Berlin, he kept in touch, too, with Hugh Dalton. Their friendship had now survived for six years, across the whole three years of King's and another three from the distances of Grantchester – London – Europe.

Dear Hugh,
    I am, as you say, dead. Further processes even have set in.
          'Though one be mild as Moses,
         His meekness clouds and closes;
          In the end he decomposes;
           And he is sure to smell.'
    As Swinburne, or you, or someone of the Romantics put it.
    I am on pretext of doing a dissertation here. Actually I have not done a word.
    I spend my time in making love to female dancers. They pirouette scornfully away . . .

After the 10th December I shall come to London. Then I shall sit one night and repeat poetry to you, and you will repeat dirty stories to me; till 8.30 a.m. Then I shall go to bed. In January I go to America for three years.

Cambridge must be full of people one knows. Perhaps it is nicer not to be there. But I am sorry not to see them capering in the Greek Play.

I have discovered the real division of mankind into the Petrine and the Jesuine; those who are crucified head downwards and those who are crucified right way up. It is immensely important. Perhaps the greatest discovery of the Twentieth Century. Beyond that I have done nothing; written but one line, but that a good one.

'Ah , love, there is no something in the sun!'

It ends a sonnet (– but what sonnet?)

It is the truest line in English except Meredith's 'And Life, some say, is worthy of the Mews.'

Be in London in December.

Rupert.

Heart, you are a restless paper scrap.

This was a line from *The Unfortunate*, one of six poems published under his name in the *Poetry Review* during his sojourn in Berlin. Another piece appearing while he was away came out in the *Cambridge Magazine*. In it, Rupert reviewed the Post-Impressionist Exhibition of Art seen at the Grafton Galleries that autumn. He paid his last of several visits there on Guy Fawkes Day, just before leaving for Berlin.

Brooke preferred the name Expressionism to Post-Impressionism and although he loved the genuine Post-Impressionists, he maintained that some of the pictures should have been in the Royal Academy, some in the New English Art Club, and a few in the muck-heap!

Twenty works of Matisse conveyed to Brooke a world 'clean, lovely and inhuman as a douche of cold water'. Picasso he considered very different and distinctly inferior, and thought that the artist did not care about colour. Picasso's two best drawings he found 'lovely and self-sufficient and inexplicable as a fugue'.

Brooke could not praise the English school much, although

approving of the seventeen year-old Stanley Spencer's 'John Donne arriving in Heaven' perhaps partly as the subject interested Brooke. He decided also that Wyndham Lewis resembled Picasso in method; that Roger Fry knew what a good picture was; and Mr Gill was one of the three or four great sculptors of the past hundred years.

Back from Berlin, Rupert branched out again into fresh interests. His first action on arrival in December was to ask Eddie Marsh if a meeting could be arranged with the Irish actress Cathleen Nesbitt, whom Brooke had admired in a play during a hectic summer's theatre-going, and remembered ever since. At the time of Rupert's requesting this meeting, Cathleen was playing Perdita in *A Winter's Tale* at the Savoy Theatre. He had actually attended the first night.

Marsh managed this in a remarkably diplomatic manner, well worthy of his political affiliations. Within forty-eight hours of Rupert's request, Marsh met Cathleen in Henry Ainley's dining room at the Savoy. By a coincidence, Miss Nesbitt also expressed to Marsh a wish to meet someone – Gilbert Cannan – so Eddie had a ready-made opportunity for organizing a supper at Raymond Buildings a week later. Its apparent purpose was to effect the meeting between Cathleen and Cannan, but quite by casual chance, Rupert Brooke was invited, too!

Eddie told Rupert of the plan, and the two of them slapped each other's backs at the way it had all been arranged.

Cathleen and Rupert found an immediate fusion of interests and sympathies. There was the obvious link of the love of the theatre; they were young and highly intelligent and both deeply devoted to poetry. Rupert fell in love with her.

'I adore you' he wrote in these and many other words. They met whenever the chance came, but both led busy lives that winter. And although she loved him too, it was not enough to want to marry him. Nevertheless, isolated, idyllic days lit their next five months.

Rupert was back at his brilliant best, and around Christmas developed a passion for the Hippodrome revue *Hello Ragtime*! He went to see it ten times altogether. Once was on New Year's Eve. After the performance, he and Marsh and some others walked down through the deserted Long Acre and Covent Garden. They passed Floral Street and the gallery entrance to the Royal Opera

House which they knew so well, and then came down to the Strand and Fleet Street, and finally on to the steps of St Paul's, where they saw in the New Year of 1913. The bells boomed out at midnight and the crowd sang *Auld Lang Syne*.

As they eventually dispersed, Rupert's party strolled the streets around Holborn, passing the row of Tudor fronts there and at long last winding a way to Raymond Buildings and the legal peace of Gray's Inn. The clock chimed three before the night was over. Yes, the inn was still gaslit, and the vestiges lingered of the old days, but now they were on the brink of a brave new world – halfway between both. Nowhere, quite, at this moment: the old year had gone, the new one come. Perhaps all was change all the time. Still so many questions, and no absolute answers. Rupert went to sleep with the safe three sides of the inn buildings sheltering him from the past and present until next day.

One of his friends of this era was St John Ervine, later the distinguished writer and playwright, but at that time a young dramatic critic. Here is his impression of Brooke, written exclusively for this book, and in his unique way.

> My memories of Rupert Brooke are few. He was still an undergraduate at Cambridge when we met for the first time, and I cannot recall just what it was that brought about our meeting. Anyhow, we became friends and, in the short time that was left to him, we saw much of him.
>
> We lived then in a charming flat on the Finchley Road, on the verge, so to speak, of the Hampstead Garden Suburb, which was a great novelty then, a daring and most attractive attempt at town planning. This flat was a meeting place for young people like ourselves, who were mostly young Fabians, as Rupert was, and very eager to put the world to rights.
>
> When Brooke came down, he lived for a while in Gray's Inn, and it was here that he met Cathleen Nesbitt, a young and very intelligent actress, who was, perhaps, too intelligent to become a celebrated player, though she became well known not only as a very capable but an absolutely trustworthy actress, who did her job well. Whether she and Rupert were ever formally engaged to be married, I don't know for certain, but there was a general impression that they were more or less engaged.

Just what Rupert meant to do in London, apart from writing poetry, I don't know. He never talked of any other work that he wished to do, and he was, we thought, tolerably well off, so he could, of course, please himself about that. Anyhow, I never heard him talk about a possible profession, and my general impression is that he meant to be a poet and only a poet.

I need not tell you what an impression Rupert made on all who saw him. The word beautiful is not one which anybody nowadays likes to apply to a man, but it is the only word that is applicable to Brooke.

I remember a night, when, returning to my flat from Fleet Street after a first night in the theatre, I was feeling fagged and out of sorts with my fellow men who lay sprawling in an ungainly heap on the seats in the Golders Green tube train. Suddenly, at Leicester Square I think (probably from the Hippodrome), the door opened and in stepped Rupert, as resplendent as a Greek god. I can't begin to tell you what his effect was. The whole carriage full of tired and sprawling and desperately dingy people lit up as if he were the sun god himself and had set fire to them.

He was an extraordinarily handsome man, very masculine in every respect, as I knew him, and with nothing in the least niminy-piminy about him. He was a male man. There is, I believe, a tendency among those who did not know him and never even saw him to think that he was effeminate. I assure you he wasn't – not in my knowledge, nor did I ever hear anybody who knew him suggest that he was.

He was a tall, robust-looking man, with broad shoulders, and he looked as if he were physically strong. His hair was golden – and I mean golden. I don't mean yellow. It looked like gold, and it shone like gold. His complexion was healthy and his eyes were bright. He was, I repeat, essentially male. How strong physically he was I do not know, but I should hate to have been his opponent in a scrap. He could, I feel, have done a good deal of damage. Such a man, one would have expected to be vain. But Rupert had no vanity that an able undergraduate ought not to have. He was modest and un-assuming, and he did not attempt to monopolise the conversation. He was not, indeed, a good talker, and could sit in company without opening his mouth. I had nearly said he was as silent as John Millington Synge, but nobody could possibly have been as silent as he was reputed to be.

As a sparkling conversationalist, then, Rupert simply did not exist. He was a young man of amazing good looks, godlike good looks, who seemed certain to be a good and perhaps even a great poet. It will not surprise me if I am told that he played games well.

The 'precious' legend is entirely false. He could, of course, do his bit of posing, like the rest of us, and take up eccentric attitudes, such as we have all at sometime assumed, but he was not conspicuously posturing or eccentric, and if he was aware of his extraordinarily handsome appearance, he never said or did anything to show that he was.

I fear that I may be making him seem a little commonplace, but that is not what I wish to do. He was exceptional in several ways, but he did not make a profession of being exceptional. I have met people with half his talent who did far more showing off in an hour than he did in the whole of my acquaintance with him. His most charming characteristic was his likeability. I suppose he had some enemies – who that has character hasn't? – but I was fortunate enough not to meet them. I'm sure I should have thought them detestable if I had!

He didn't like London. 'The dreadful state of busied indolence London reduces me to, stops me from ever carrying out any intent, or doing anything' he wrote to my wife in an undated letter, 'I have done no work in the last fortnight . . .'

On a postcard – he was addicted to postcards – he writes 'I'm sorry to be so incompetent. London life is too much for me.' On another, he says 'There is a nightmare of a fog which makes me feel ill. I hate London!'

One evening in January, St John Ervine dined with Rupert, Cathleen and Marsh, and then the three men went on to one of the classic Shaw-Belloc debates. Later still, back at Raymond Buildings, Rupert read his completed *Lithuania* to them.

When Cathleen Nesbitt and Rupert first met, she was still getting over a very recent relationship with actor Henry Ainley, while

Rupert was recovering from the Ka Cox affair. Rupert called Cathleen 'incredibly, inordinately, devastatingly, immortally, calamitously, hearteningly, adorably beautiful'.

They saw *Hello Ragtime* revue half a dozen times together. At this period, Rupert had been lent a flat in Thurloe Square, London. One Sunday when she visited him there, she had a toothache and he tucked her up on the sofa with an aspirin washed down with hot milk. They knew they were in love. I adore you, Rupert wrote to her. The four months to April 1913 were blurred into a 'colourful kaleidoscope' as Cathleen put it.

They often used to take a train into the country and go for long walks holding hands. They would make these trips on Sundays and Mondays. If they spent the night at an inn, they occupied separate rooms. Rupert sat on her bed and they talked into the small hours – but they did not become lovers. Nor did they live in an 'exalted atmosphere' perpetually, but Rupert's spirits inspired Cathleen 'with a kind of vitality and gaiety which was not really in my nature' as she expressed it in her autobiography (*A Little Love and Good Company*, published by Faber & Faber).

So the whirl went round and round. Rupert and Geoffrey Keynes saw Cathleen Nesbitt acting in *General John Regan.* And at other times, Brooke met many of the most promising people of the day: D.H. Lawrence, Granville-Barker, Rose Macaulay, James Barrie, Robert Bridges and the Georgian poets. Through Eddie Marsh he also got to know the Asquiths, George Wyndham, and the Bernard Shaws.

Eddie Marsh observed a gradual change in Brooke's outlook, perhaps dating from the late Grantchester period, and accentuated after his illness of 1912: a shift he described as Brooke's discovery that goodness was the most important thing in life – 'that immortal beauty and goodness' as Rupert wrote later.

Brooke still felt the urge to get right away from the London – and even the English – scene, but he went on enjoying himself for the first few months of the year. He had an appetite for any show or play at all – and the Russian Ballet he visited whenever they came. It was the gallery or pit for these expeditions, as although he had a private allowance, it was not enough for extravagance. The ballet he interspersed with another dose of ragtime.

He indulged in this last London fling, as he knew that sooner or later he would be off to America and possibly beyond. This was the sort of life one could only lead for a limited time. Everything happened at such an endless, remorseless pace that he would crack eventually. Yet although he pleaded that it left no time for serious study or composition, several poems emerged from this pre-travel period of early 1913.

Elated at having won a £30 prize offered by *Poetry Review* for the best poem of 1912 in that publication, he and Cathleen celebrated suitably with some other friends. Elated, yes; but not conceited, for he felt several others were better than his own.

By now, new poems and prose had been accepted by various journals as well as his regulars. *The Night Journey*, for instance, in *Rhythm*, with its imaginative impressions of a train leaving a station, and all the mingled emotions it aroused. Rupert was always travelling in a train of thought, forever aiming at elusive lands: happy, restless, wondering. The constant search for the perfect place, for ecstasy. He wrote in a line from an unpublished sonnet:

Love soars from earth to ecstasies unwist

Then back to earth again to an imaginary Cambridgeshire folk-song invented by Brooke while staying with Jacques and Gwen Raverat at the village of Croydon-cum-Clopton. Clopton does not now exist, he explained, the inhabitants having been wiped out by the Black Death. How did it come to be told to Rupert? Allegedly by his taking it down from the Clopton blacksmith. So there was still a lot of boyish nonsense in Brooke, now at the age of twenty-five. Before his next birthday, he told friends he would not now marry, as he was too old.

On 8 March he was finally awarded his Fellowship at Cambridge, but overlooked the actual date and had to send a telegram of apology for absence. Next week, however, he remembered to go there to be admitted or 'churched' as he termed it. Then the following day he caught the famous 4.55 p.m. train back to town again. Many times he had travelled on this train in his undergraduate and later days, as it reached London in time for the evening shows or dinner. He saw it as an old, trusted friend that stayed the same in a shifting world – and got him to town by around seven o'clock!

The Fellowship thesis on John Webster was subsequently reviewed as showing 'a scholarship remarkable in one so young'. Brooke received many messages congratulating him on the honour, which he did not take at all seriously. One of these came from John Masefield, at Well Walk. Masefield mentions, too, that Granville-Barker was very interested in Brooke's play, and urged him to continue writing drama.

Rupert used to devote almost all day to meeting his various London friends at this time, which necessitated sending a steady stream of postcards all over the place to organize these arrangements. He augmented his correspondence by the still-novel telephone, invaluable with the intricate timing often involved. It is these surviving scraps of day-to-day notes, strangely enough, which make the most poignant impact of all on an observer.

Just about March, he wrote his sonnet *Love*, starting

Love is a breach in the walls, a broken gate

And on the back of the rough manuscript is written, in Brooke's hasty hand, two notes to remind him of these routine rendezvous. One reads simply '49 Bedford Square at 11.30' and the other 'T. S. M. Well Walk Tuesday'. The latter was presumably Thomas Sturge Moore. How tragically trivial these jottings seem, buried on the back of a library manuscript, yet they are as real and alive as his poems and letters: evidence of the life he led, knowledge that he was in certain places at actual times.

And the little human touches, too. In his sad *Song*, for instance, with its verse:

Love came our quiet way
Lit pride in us, and died in us,
All in a winter's day.
There is no more to say.

Rupert's original pale pencil handwriting bears a semi-colon after 'lit pride in us' and not a comma.

More arrangements, this time Brooke and Drinkwater were to visit a theatre, but as Rupert was invited as the guest, he wrote urgently asking how he should be dressed. Normally he would have worn his individual Norfolk jacket and flannels attire, but he did not want to embarrass Drinkwater. He was very relieved to learn that anything would be acceptable – and evening dress was not necessary! After the play, they stayed up most of the night talking poetry, the Georgian venture, literature, and life in general.

Georgian Poetry 1911–12 included five of Brooke's best poems from this period: *The Old Vicarage, Grantchester; Dust; The Fish; Town and Country; Dining Room Tea*. They had a lot to discuss, for the first edition sold out virtually on the date of publication, so that a second one had been started. The Prime Minister was one of the first purchasers.

Maurice Hewlett told Eddie Marsh that Brooke was truly a poet, regarding Rupert, W.H. Davies and Walter de la Mare as the best three in the book. Others were to be hardly less noted, however: Masefield himself, Alfred Noyes, Newbolt, James Elroy Flecker, Wilfred Gibson, Sturge Moore. Quite a constellation. A new movement had been born, given expression: alert, alive, anti-Victorian, anti-Edwardian, pro-Georgian. Essentially of the twentieth century, and forward looking, seeking fresh forms. But how little was the way ahead that some of them could look in the spring of 1913. . .

Yet the spring came promptly, and Rupert wrote ecstatically of it to Cathleen from his home at Rugby, yearning 'to walk 1000 miles, and write 1000 plays, and sing 1000 poems, and drink 1000 pots of beer, and kiss 1000 girls'. The spring, he concluded, made him almost ill with excitement.

His trip grew nearer, although the financial hurdle was not quite topped, as he could only rake together about £200. Meanwhile, he kept up his contributions to periodicals. For *Poetry and Drama* he wrote on the poems of John Donne. And to the *Blue Review* he sent two poems, *Love* and *The Busy Heart*, with its opening line:

Now that we've done our best and worst, and parted

And a final article before leaving revealed that in his opinion, *Appius and Virginia*, although attributed to John Webster, was not actually his work. Brooke had twenty copies of this reprinted and several survive.

So spring reached London, too, as the trees of Gray's Inn

coloured the drab brick façades, and daisies dotted its lawns with white. Rupert had moved to South Kensington now, but was still in the thick of the social whirl. At last the chance came for his travels to turn into reality, chief credit for this being due to a girl named Naomi Royde-Smith. For several years, she had been an admirer of Brooke's verse and she was delighted to see some of it published in the *Westminster Gazette*, where she worked.

In 1912, she graduated to the literary editorship of the weekly and met Rupert for the first time. She became fond of him at once, and when she discovered he wanted a drastic change of scene – preferably in the New World – she managed to persuade her editor to commission a series of articles on America and Canada from first-hand experience. Rupert was more than ready for such an opportunity, which meant that he need not worry so much about the money aspect. And by then, he had wearied of London's endless activity in a circle revolving to no visible effect. It had all become a bit too precious for Rupert, who never aspired to society for its own social sake.

He jumped at the chance to cross the Atlantic and write a series of weekly impressions of what he saw. No strings attached; he could go anywhere, report anything. It all seemed too good to be true. So in April, from the elegance of South Kensington, he started preparing with enthusiastic thoroughness – from letters of introduction to guide books and extra clothes.

'London for me won't do' he said.

All his poems this spring seemed not surprisingly to be on severance of love ties, light or grave or both. *The Chilterns* has touches of sophisticated humour and then there comes this:

> What's left behind I shall not find
> The splendour and the pain
> The splash of sun, the shouting wind,
> And the brave sting of rain,
> I may not meet again.

On 15 April Rupert went to the birthday party of Violet Asquith, who told him of various friends he should visit in New York.

Then when it got to the final four weeks, Brooke found he had too much left to do. He saw Cathleen as often as possible; sometimes for tea in her dressing room, or when she was ill in late April, at her home. With the days dwindling, they thought only of there and then.

He started on a wide round of farewells in May. First to Eddie Marsh, who was leaving London before Brooke on a Mediterranean cruise. Next he sent *Lithuania* to John Drinkwater in case it could be staged during his absence.

Then suddenly the last day dawned. A pale, precious morning, lightening delicately over Kensington. He was still rushing around arranging last-night meetings, and he sent a scrawled note by hand to a friend from his home at 5 Thurloe Square:

May 20th

I'm very sorry, I live in a whirl of mismanagement and incompetence. I'm engaged here all day. But from 10 p.m. till midnight, I'm going to sink beer in the restaurant under Gambrinus, Regent Street. Gibson and one or two others will be drifting in and out.

And from 11.40 to 12 tomorrow I shall be dissolved in tears on the platform at Euston. At 12 my train starts. If you're near either of these places, do look in, if only for a moment. If you appear tonight, I will ply you with grilled kidneys. If I don't see you ever, in aeternium vale. Remember me to Locke Ellis.

R.B.

John Middleton Murry was one of those friends he saw on the evening of 20 May. Murry, working as a journalist and reviewer, wrote from Chancery Lane to Katherine Mansfield that day:

'I'm going to supper with Rupert tonight because he's going off to America in the morning; it's all very silly, but a free meal is fascinating.'

Later Murry said that his own touch of resentment was plain to see. There was nothing at all silly in Rupert's going to America, nor in his asking Murry to a parting supper. Murry was merely envious, as he remained a slave, while Brooke was free.

The evening went down in memory as one of those rarely magic moments when all is entranced, sharpened, by the proximity of parting. It was early morning before Rupert arrived back at Thurloe Square for a few hours' sleep in the tall grey house. Then next day, to Euston, Liverpool, and the New World.

In May, Rupert started the sonnet *Mutability*. It must be the poem composed over the two most distant points possible: begun in a quiet square in South Kensington, finished at Makaweli in the South Seas.

Poor straws! on the dark flood we catch awhile.

Mutability, in a world of change.

Chapter Nine

To America and Canada

Brooke boarded the SS *Cedric* and was led along to his cabin, number 50. His cases had already arrived, and he looked at their initials RCB unconsciously, then raised his eyes to the porthole. Framed in its circle he saw Birkenhead across the Mersey. He had an early evening meal and retired.

22 May opened with grey skies. The sight of so many people on the quayside to see off friends depressed him suddenly with a sense of solitude. On an impulse, Brooke hopped ashore down the main gangway, found a lad called William who was there just for interest, and pressed sixpence into the palm of his small hand on the understanding that the boy would wave to Brooke until the ship slid clear of the quay! The lad carried out his part of the pact faithfully, even shouting spontaneities quite inaudible to Brooke up on deck. Rupert, in turn, returned the waving and felt less alone as the *Cedric* set course westward.

East-scudding clouds presaged a choppy day or two, as the cranes and wharves and sprawl of the Mersey moved from sight, the Irish coast faded, and nothing but water lay between the *Cedric* and the Statue of Liberty.

Someone told Brooke that the poet Richard le Galliene and his wife were also aboard, but he remained unimpressed with them and did not strike an acquaintance. His first friendship on the vessel was thrust at him by a hearty New-Century, New-World Canadian girl who kept trying to lead him into deserted corners of the ship – around lifeboats and similar spots – and then attempted to teach him her national anthem! If this failed, she did succeed in getting across to him a more frivolous ditty boasting these memorable lyrics:

> Splash me! Splash me! Splash me with the ocean blue.
> Mash me! Mash me! and I promise that I'll mash you.

This unnerving episode occurred within the first few days out from Liverpool, and although it amused Brooke, he was glad to get back to the safety of cabin 50. So this was a product of the New World youth. Somewhat more shattering than Newnhamites.

He also met a Mr Klaw, who expressed a passionate interest in theatre, so Rupert expanded his ideas on the drama and discovered that the man had major connections with several New York theatres.

Now all idea of time seemed lost and here in mid-ocean unfolded a new world – as there was to be at the other end.

The sense of strangeness which he felt, with horizons surrounding him right round the compass, was underlined by some exotically fresh dishes, too, including the colourfully-named clam chowder. The prospect of this food spurred Brooke to concoct a Swinburnesque lyric for a letter to Cathleen Nesbitt, which went along these lines:

> If you were like clam-chowder
> And I were like the spoon,
> And the band were playing louder
> And a little more in tune,
> I'd stir you till I spilled you,
> Or kiss you till I killed you,
> If you were like clam-chowder
> And I were like the spoon.

Rupert Brooke and New York. Something at once apt and yet incongruous about the two together. Already he had tasted the American outlook, for a US youth on board had practically insisted on reciting the Declaration of Independence to him.

The initial impact of the New York scene from the ship surprised and inspired Brooke. The vessel passed the Statue as evening fell, and slowly steaming in, he saw Brooklyn Bridge, over which 'luminous trams, like shuttles of fire, are thrown across and across, continually weaving the stuff of human existence'. In the fading sky he glimpsed 'the low golden glare of Coney Island,' while 'a few streamers of smoke flew over the city, oblique and parallel, pennants of our civilisation'.

Rupert read into the clusters of skyscrapers some purpose and greatness beyond their mere convenience. Here were symbols of the century, clutching towards heaven in a ragged group. This was a moment in a million. Sundown, and the restless triumphant skyline silhouetted, each spire studded with a stream of lights challenging the stars. And then, looking down into the water reflecting the remnants of this summer day, he suddenly saw that New York was real, it lived, and people breathed there, for floating refuse of every kind bobbed against the hull of the ship as she edged in closer to this city of dreams – broken and real.

Yes, to the city. Rupert at large in New York, not probing too deep, just content to look and listen. The sidewalks with people chewing gum, their jaws forever moving; the security of Fifth Avenue; the floodlit toothbrush ads; the theatres, the movies, the elevated trains, the cars. These were what he saw, what anyone would see. Yet he observed them more closely and at the same time with detachment.

And the New Yorkers themselves – what of them? The preference of belts to braces; men not ashamed to walk about in their shirtsleeves; the latest fashion creations of Bakst; and the wonders of the department store. And most of all, he noticed that scarcely any English – or American – was heard in the streets.

He was not completely captivated by New York. Its commercialism appalled him: the undertaker who included for seventy-five dollars 'everything that the most morbid taphologist could suggest including four draped flambeaux'!

E.S.P. Haynes gave Brooke several introductions to friends in America – one being a Swedenborgian railway king well over eighty years old! Haynes wondered at the time whether the former Swede would appreciate Rupert. He need not have worried, though, for although the two were together no more than twenty-four hours, Brooke must have made an unusual impression, for a letter from the old man to Haynes after Brooke's death showed that the Swede regarded it as a real tragedy.

Brooke wrote to Eddie Marsh, then in the Greek Islands, that New York was 'a gritty refuse-heap of reality'. He could not comprehend Greece just then, and London itself seemed a dream. Meanwhile, he went on exploring the sights, and decided that apart from revues, the stage shows were not exciting. No wonder Klaw had been over in London looking for fresh plays.

One day in early June he passed in the country outside the metropolis flirting with a girl named Louise, but apart from one or two such encounters, he found New York a little lonely. So in mid-month he took a boat trip down the coast to Boston. Here he was struck by the simple truth that it is often far better to get a first or last impression of a place from the sea, rather than by rail. It was certainly so with Boston, as he watched it rising on its little hills, and looking civilized and homely after New York for all its impact. In Boston, too, he found life leisured with time for real hospitality. And still it lived, although already New York had replaced it as the leading American city in the arts. Boston was nearly to New York what Munich was to Berlin. Both had been the leaders forty years before.

And across the river from Boston – Cambridge, Massachusetts. How could he ignore it, distant as it seemed from King's in sense and space and all dimensions? Brooke reached Cambridge, more particularly Harvard, in the University's Commencement – Eights Week and May Week and everything else in one. Here he met people he understood, a young-in-heart group with 'the charm and freshness and capacity for instantly creating a relation of happy and warm friendliness'.

The climax of the celebrations was that annual ritual, the Harvard-Yale baseball game. He settled in his seat and watched amazed the knickerbockered players, hot under the June sky; and then he saw America pass in review. The graduates of every year marched past the stands, from the 1850s down to 1912. Brooke asked a companion why there seemed to be no-one between about fifty and sixty. The reply was simply: 'The war'.

However young this country and the university actually was, Brooke sensed 'something terrifying in the completeness of their lives and their civilisation . . . like a company of dons whose studies are of a remote and finished world'. But the subject of their scholarship was the nineteenth century and especially Victorian England.

112

Brooke was not unduly surprised when asked if he had known Matthew Arnold, and avoided explaining that Arnold died when he was exactly eight months old!

Brooke's literary output in the month he spent in New York and Boston amounted to notes for four weekly letters, to be written later for the *Westminster Gazette*, and eight lonely lines of verse, *There's a Wisdom in Women*. This could be sold for a guinea, he told Marsh in a covering letter.

On the last day but one in June, he left America for Canada; 'a country without a soul' American friends warned him, when they heard of his intention. But defying these cries, he took the Montreal Express out of New York at 7.45 p.m. on the night of the 29th.

As usual, Rupert had rushed round the city saying farewell to the friends he had made there, so ate nothing all day. Only as the train exploded out of the station did he discover that it had no restaurant car aboard, and his last memory of the United States for almost a year was munching an orange and feeling almost starving after it. With the sweet tang still in his mouth, he clambered gracefully in a lofty sleeping berth directly over an old lady who was snoring almost before the train crossed the Hudson River.

Then propped up in bed, he pulled back one of the two little curtains at the window, relaxed back on to his elbow, and peeped into the black night. Faintly he made out the surface of a large lake lying away behind the trees. It was all strange beyond belief. Glimpses of shapes and places he had never seen, nor ever would. The world was passing him by in darkness. At last he tired of looking out towards the racing landscape and thought of the more familiar sights. He started a letter to Eddie Marsh, barely legible with the motion of the train, and spoke in fun of his mental stupor in America. The pace and the people apparently did not inspire any lasting lyrics. Perhaps it was all too far away; or not far enough.

The night wore away, and in the early hours Brooke fell fitfully asleep, as the express raced round the clock and crossed into Canada. Then a miracle. Early next morning, as he was grappling to get his trousers on in an upper berth, he pulled a curtain open again to see the train running beside a huge sunlit river, the splendid St Lawrence curving crystal blue in the sparkling new day. Everything had changed. It was a world – not just a night – away from New York. But soon the outlook switched to squalor as the poorer parts of Montreal blurred row and row past the window.

Rupert set out to see Montreal by wagonette observation-car in company with a score of tourists, and found an 'atmospheric' similarity to Glasgow. A city of banks and churches, he found it terribly tedious and delayed only a day or two.

He would be going on to Ottawa soon, but before this, he caught the night boat from Montreal to Quebec. The vessel left the gloom of Montreal and swung into the sweeping St Lawrence. On board, Brooke met a middle-aged American Jew, also travelling more or less aimlessly. This man said everything he thought, but despite his transparent mind he became an agreeable companion to Rupert for a day or two. They awoke after the night on the river to a perfect midsummer morning, and there high above stood the citadel of Quebec, dominant on its headland in the course of the water. A youthful city, he saw it, with 'the radiance and repose of an immortal'.

Rupert took a calèche, a little local two-wheeled carriage, and together with the American, he saw where Wolfe fell, and all the other points of historic renown. The American burst into a slightly off-key rendering of 'The Star-Spangled Banner' as they jogged past his national consulate! Soon he settled down to sleep, while the carriage rocked them along narrower and still narrower streets paved with planks.

Brooke liked it here. Alone, on another day, he paused on Dufferin Terrace to sit and stare at the Lower Town, backed by the river, the citadel, and the Isle of Orleans. 'Hour by hour, the colours change, and sunlight follows shadow, and mist rises, and smoke drifts across.' He also wrote to Eddie Marsh from this perfect point close to the House of Parliament. When a man and two girls came and sat nearby, he had 'a slight lust' for one of them as she looked so graceful and neat in the red and white outfit.

But once more the colours changed, the moment passed.

He took another river trip which he had been recommended: 130 miles down the St Lawrence, ninety miles up a tributary, the Saguenay, and then back to Quebec. After passing a host of tiny French hamlets alongside the river, the boat finally reached the junction with the Saguenay. The St Lawrence here is twenty miles wide, and the boat turned into the tributary during darkness, so that the narrowness and the night combined to convey an oppressive sense to the dim outlines of vast cliffs following their course.

Back at the junction of the rivers again, Brooke stopped for a day at the village there called Tadousac. In this remote spot, he felt the full desolation of the river which faded out of sight across its wide span. The sun beat down hotly, so Rupert stripped off his clothes, hesitated a second, and plunged in. Despite the summer, the water was icy. He swam for only a couple of minutes, before striking back to land and scrambling on to the hot rocks. He patted himself dry with a handkerchief, dressed and ran all the way back to the little log hotel, still shivering, his hair gleaming gold in the sunlight.

At Ottawa, the money motive was not all. Here Brooke sensed more civilized surroundings than Montreal, where statistics and size had seemed much more important to the people than art or culture. Even at Ottawa, however, he felt unable to record fine, clear impressions. He had visualized himself composing at a prolific rate once he was 'dancing through foreign cities' but the brain did not respond! The normally sensitive reactions were not forthcoming. Still, he liked the grace of Ottawa and the soft Canadian accents heard in its streets. And one considerable compensation was the hospitality shown to him by the Canadian poet Duncan Campbell Scott.

John Masefield had given Brooke a letter of introduction to Scott, and also to the Canadian Prime Minister, Sir Wilfred Laurier, with whom he lunched. But it was Scott who really entertained Brooke for the next week. Rupert was registered at an Ottawa hotel, but spent all the time at Scott's home. Although the Canadian was twice Brooke's age, they got along well, with poetry in common, and were photographed together in the garden. Scott wore rimless spectacles and sat in a modern-looking broad-striped summer chair, with a kitten in his lap, while Rupert balanced a teacup on the wide arm of a wooden chair. Brooke, for once, wore a high wing collar, and his hair fell over his forehead towards his left eye.

He took most of his meals either with the Scotts or at the Royal Ottawa Golf Club, and as the week passed he grew less lonely than when he had reached the capital. They coaxed him to read poems from *Georgian Poetry* and his own recent work, and discussed literature at length with him.

Scott thought Brooke not only handsome, but that everything

about him went together harmoniously. His last memory of the eight days Brooke spent in Ottawa was typical: Rupert lying on his back on the rug in Scott's library playing with the kitten, who had the name of Skokum.

And before Brooke said adieu, he took Scott to the Golf Club house for drinks. Here with whisky and soda, they toasted poetry, for Rupert described Scott as 'the only poet in Canada'. As the Canadian was to visit England in the autumn, Rupert wrote to friends asking them to welcome him appropriately.

Just before leaving Ottawa, Brooke took a twenty-mile excursion out of it by motor car over dusty tracks to a lovely lake in the hills away to the north-west. Beside the rough road grew mildweed, cornflowers, thimbleberry blossom, and purple-red fireweed. He breathed air as clear and clean as the visibility, and felt excited, elated, that the North Pole lay straight ahead with scarcely any civilization between it and him.

With that thought, he returned to Ottawa, but only to take to the water once more for his next call – Toronto. The boat picked a channel through the famous Thousand Isles, but 'each, if big enough, has been bought by a rich man – generally an American – who has built a castle on it. So the whole isn't much more beautiful than Golders Green.'

Toronto at last, on the shores of the lake. But the unfortunate people scarcely saw it as the waterfront was occupied by smoke, stores, railways and wharves.

Despite this prospect, Rupert noted here the beginnings of art. But only the beginnings. The first repertory theatre in Canada, he prophesied, would be founded in Toronto some thirty years hence, and would daringly present *Candida* and *The Silver Box*!

What can one say about Toronto? 'It is impossible to give it anything but commendation. It is not squalid like Birmingham, or cramped like Canton, or scattered like Edmonton, or sham like Berlin, or hellish like New York, or tiresome like Nice. It is all right. The only depressing thing is that it will always be what it is, only larger, and that no Canadian city can ever be anything better or different. If they are good they may become Toronto.'

Despite this penetrating analysis, Brooke felt some sympathy for the place. Duncan Scott gave him an introduction to the Arts and Letters Club, where he met men who were very kind to him. Two of them bore the homely names of Morris and McTavish. Edmund Morris, a noted painter of Indians, shepherded Brooke to the Club, then housed in the old Assize Court of Toronto. A poetry lover, Rufus Hathaway, at the club that first night had already read Rupert's poems in *Georgian Poetry* and another man owned a copy of his *Poems*. Awful triumph, Brooke told Marsh.

'You're better than Alfred Noyes, in my opinion,' someone else volunteered.

So here among artists, poets and journalists, Brooke felt more at home than in any other city so far. He wrote regularly to no-one now, not even his 'four young women' – presumably the Olivier girls. Noel and the New Forest seemed centuries ago, if it ever happened, and even Cathleen Nesbitt filled his mind less. A strange, complicated thing was life. Not so simple just to be happy. Perhaps the most elusive of all. Next day, he set out from the King Edward Hotel, Toronto, for the wilds and the West: Winnipeg and on to Vancouver. But first he had to see Niagara.

Two days later, writing to Marsh from the Clifton Hotel, Niagara, he described the falls as low and broad and gloomy. Then with typical originality of thought, he said he was hearing the same noise as George Washington only a little later on. The hotels, bridges, trams, postcards, sideshows and all the touts of all kinds there, he deplored deeply. Then he admitted the power of the falls, and that 'he who sees them instantly forgets humanity'. Brooke watched the spray, ranging from diaphanous to dark, and thought of the river of life, with many flashing moments within a single stream.

By boat now, through Lakes Huron and Superior. On the Sunday the journey started, they passed picnic parties and others ashore looking so happy that Brooke felt the way of life here had a fine breezy, enviable healthiness. Then the boat moved past a small canoe with a red-shirted man and a bronzed girl. The voyagers whistled, sang, and shouted 'Snooky ookums' to the pair, much to Rupert's amusement.

He was sitting next to an old lady on deck who would raise a massive telescope to her eye every few minutes, aim it at a distant shore, and if she saw signs of life there, wave her tiny handkerchief – though no-one could possibly have seen it at that range!

Ashore again, and by night train in a lower sleeping berth, he got

117

between the sheets, pulled up the blinds a few inches, and watched the woods and hills of the wild starlit landscape make a mingled night of dream and reality. And early next morning, the train roared into Winnipeg and the West.

Here he found 'a tempered democracy' and architecture more hideous than in the east, 'but cheerily and windily so'. Western manners seemed better than east, in compensation.

The wilds suited him better than Winnipeg itself, so he found a friend and headed for a far-off lodge at Lake George, seventy miles north. Here in the wilderness and waste, he mused that no-one else was thinking of the lakes and hills he saw before him. They had no tradition, these places, often no names. All was still virginal, untrodden, rare. Dawn followed sunset with an infinite loneliness – and a loveliness, too.

He was here on his twenty-sixth birthday, lying naked on a beach of golden sand. He lay and thought and remembered. The past was over. The future unreal. And the present? This should have meant something. But did it? What was the meaning of it all? Back at the hunting lodge, he wrote to Cathleen telling her how they had landed at a place which was an Indian camp. The complete contrast, from Brooke in the backwoods of Manitoba, to Cathleen Nesbitt in her Shaftesbury Avenue world.

Pressing westwards, on relentlessly to Regina. The children in the same carriage kept on demanding: How many inches to Regina? A billion? A trillion? A shillion? Past the Prairies, vast, vastly lonely.

Two other passengers in the corner argued about the merits and size of their respective home-towns of Edmonton and Calgary. Each vied with the other about the rate of growth. Then for a change one of them turned to Rupert and asked:

'Say, where do you come from, friend?'

Rupert had to admit to them that Grantchester, having numbered 300 at the time of Julius Caesar, and risen to nearly 400 by Domesday Book, had now dropped to 350 in the year of grace 1913. They seemed 'perplexed and angry', Rupert reported!

By 13 August, he was at Edmonton, three-quarters across Canada, where he wrote telling Eddie Marsh that he had become the complete journalist, demanding free passes and bursting in on people for interviews.

Back in the east, he had been regarded as a poet, but three days later at Calgary he was a political expert – and reporters started interviewing him! Columns appeared in the local papers reporting his opinions on the situation in Europe and other topics. Brooke told Marsh that he would demand a knighthood from Winston when he came back!

From Calgary, Rupert saw the Rockies rising seventy miles away. 'They are irrelevant to humanity' he concluded. 'No recorded Hannibal has ever struggled across them; nor is their story in any remembered literature.'

On again, towards these giants. Sitting in the observation car at the rear of the train westward, he likened this carriage to life, when you never saw the glories until they were past. Through the Rockies themselves. But Banff he found ordinary, though beautiful enough.

Yet Lake Louise was another world. Here in the Selkirk mountains, amid milky green waters reflecting peaks and pines, he met an alluring widow – the Lady of the Chateau – who helped him to pass an idyllic few days. So it was people not places that really mattered.

Across the Great Divide, and there at last lay Vancouver, surrounded by mountains and with an air of the Orient about it. Passing south to the States and San Francisco, he discovered with alarm that he had lost his precious notebook containing all the impressions of his Canadian travels, so he could do little except write the rest of the articles for the *Westminster Gazette* from memory. The American ones had been safely dispatched earlier.

September sped by in the friendly setting of Berkeley University, where he found himself positively revered, not for his own abilities so much as his associations with such legendary Englishmen as John Masefield. Names like these seemed unbelievably remote to the students at Berkeley, a continent and an ocean away from England.

Brooke liked California and the easy companionship of a young state. San Francisco was just recovering from the fire of '06 and everything looked new and touched with gold. Meanwhile, he took this opportunity to clear up his affairs in case he decided to go still further into the unexplored. Any completed poems he posted to Marsh, and half-finished ones he hoped to find peace to finish.

In a note to Dr Dent, Brooke was still wondering whether to go on or not, as he thought of Cambridge, 'that lovely grey city of ours'. Eventually, he tossed a coin to decide: heads for home, tails for the Pacific. He flicked an American dollar into the air, caught it in one hand, and slowly uncovered his fingers to see which it would be. There it was in his hand – tails.

So on 1 October, he wrote to Eddie Marsh saying that he would be sailing for Honolulu in a few days, and suggested himself in the centre of a Gauguin picture nakedly riding a squat horse into white surf: how lucky the coin came down right, or he would never have written his poems from the South Seas.

Chapter Ten

Westward to the South Seas

The ship sailed south-west from 'Frisco, and all at once the utter remoteness of the Pacific swept over Rupert. As if the world were flat and they were early voyagers heading towards its edge, not knowing where or when they might see land again.

Among the passengers were some Hawaiians returning home, who gave him a foretaste of the South Seas with their background music of soft-slumbrous love-songs, chanted to chords from strings on the mild autumn air. Several of the Hawaiian girls looked longingly at the strangely beautiful Englishman, but he had not yet succumbed to the mesmeric charm of the islands.

During these first few days and nights that the ship cut calmly through the Pacific, Rupert wrote two of his South Seas poems: the sonnets *He Wonders Whether* and *Clouds*. The former had no particular connection with the place or period except that he said:

I have peace to weigh your worth, now all is over,

But *Clouds* was a direct inspiration from communion with the Pacific skies. Accomplished as much of his previous work was, this marked a new degree of mastery over the sonnet, with its exquisite opening lines:

Down the blue night the unending columns press
In noiseless tumult, break and wave and flow,

Two thousand miles, and Honolulu about the middle of the month. And from here, he sent a small group of poems to Eddie Marsh, four of which were at once re-directed to *Poetry and Drama*: *He Wonders Whether*; *Clouds*; *The Funeral of Youth*; and *The Way that Lovers Use*. So the two sonnets he had written in early October on the other side of the world reached home and appeared in print within two months of their conception.

Honolulu seemed terribly Americanized to Brooke, who could not enthuse over it. Nevertheless, from Waikiki Beach, where he stayed for some days, he wrote two more sonnets, suggesting that a surrender to the Islands must have begun. From one:

> Somewhere before the dawn I rose, and stept
> Softly along the dim way to your room,

And in Waikiki—

> Somewhere an eukaleli thrills and cries
> And stabs with pain the night's brown savagery;

He had tasted the pure pagan life and it appealed to him, for there ran a strong vein of the primitive in his highly sensitive makeup. This was another world, he was discovering, infinitely different from England and all civilization. The barriers were down, inhibitions gone. Yet he was torn between the two; he had not yet let go. And *One Day* wrote,

> Today I have been happy. All the day

remembering the past in England.

They crossed the Equator near Phoenix Islands, and another few days brought them to Samoa. He had sent nine articles back to the *Westminster Gazette* before leaving San Francisco; now he was too engrossed, engulfed, with the wonder of the South Seas to do more.

It was all true what they said about these parts. The heaven here on earth; lovely natives; tropic climate; perfect settings. He fell for the thatched roofs of the homes, and the palms dark against the morning light. From a Samoan grass hut he wrote to Cathleen, who was still

> Lucretia, Helen, Mary, in one breath!

122

Brooke saw the lithe grace of the girls, a beautiful brown free from any 'Melanesian admixture'. He told Denis Browne that he was becoming more and more Robert Louis Stephenson, and at this stage actually wondered when or even if he would ever return north again. While at Samoa, he made a pilgrimage to Stephenson's grave at Vailima, where the Scotsman had been buried nineteen years earlier.

Brooke became bronzed and tough, and life was one long picnic. Yet even at the outposts, he saw the signs of civilization. At a remote village, one of the chiefs possessed a passion for collecting pictures from *The Sketch*! He used to cut out illustrations and nail them to the beams of his hut, which was thus decorated with a strange assortment of fashion photos, a golf champion in the act of driving, and portraits of stage and social celebrities. And in one of the copies, Rupert came across a picture of Cathleen. London to Samoa. Now as he looked at her cultured beauty, it was the periodical and all its world which seemed unreal. Did it actually exist? London, fogs, King's, Cathleen, Eddie Marsh. Were they all living their lives away this very moment? It must be so, yet the reality seemed much more here, in this hut on a Samoan beach, where the sun blazed and the surf played perpetually the song of peace.

At last, saturated with Samoa, he moved on from its coconuts and waterfalls to Fiji, where to his utter disgust he found a flourishing township complete with bookmakers! Despite this temporary interruption to the primitive paganism, Brooke was realizing reluctantly the dangers as well as the delights of a soporific Pacific existence. He felt afraid at times that he would stop serious thought altogether soon, and already he had expressed a preference for a siva-siva dance to Nijinski. Six men and six girls, naked to the waist, against an exciting background of flaming torches, moving to plangent rhythms under the stars.

So to Suva, with its hibiscus wreaths for the hair, the sleek canoes threading through depth-clear waters with their turtles and tropical fish. Brooke had an attachment to water, whether the chuckling mill at Grantchester, or the Fijian sea. And it was while here that he completed that little satiric cameo *Heaven*, a fishy paradise where,

There shall be no more land, say Fish.

On 1 December 1913, while at McDonald's Hotel, Suva, he had his first real yearnings to be home. Later they subsided for several months. As a way out of his dilemma, he was evolving a pattern of life when he could live a quarter of each year with Jacques and Gwen Raverat, Dudley and Anne Ward, the Ranee (Mrs Brooke), and the last three months alone. Won't 1914 be fun, he ended a letter. . . But he was still sufficiently happy here, so the dilemma remained.

When he was content – most of the time – he would adorn his letters with sketches such as the one to Denis Browne, the musician. In it, he depicted himself sitting on top of the world, while Browne, in a blackened area, hammered away at the keys in the underworld of England at the bottom of the globe. Then in mock-sadder mood, he splashed the sheets with 'tear-stains' denoting how he felt to be away from friends. What were his real feelings? A mixture some way between these two poles.

In the early part of December, he was among the angry mountains of Fiji, buffeted by thunderstorms, threatened by volcanoes. By the middle of the month, he was departing – to the sincere sorrow of many of the people there, who had been as usual attracted by his charm. One of the friends he had made was a towering native guide, Ambele, who wore only a loin cloth and a giant grin.

The last outward port of call came now. Auckland at its midsummer, a week before Christmas. Rupert ate dishes of strawberries, feeling as if it were some ghastly perversion or sin! The country of New Zealand impressed him only as rather dull and grey after the tropic-strong shades of the Islands. And despite the Liberal or Fabian way of life, it still seemed very much less than paradise – in fact, far worse than the natural anarchy of the Pacific. Which was better? Things got perplexing sometimes. Meanwhile, he had two or three weeks before a boat was due to take him to Tahiti. He tidied up one or two poems already roughed out, and enclosed a couple on 16 January when he next wrote to Marsh, from Tahiti. These were *Heaven* and the immortal sonnet

> Not with vain tears, when we're beyond the sun,
> We'll beat on the substantial doors, nor tread
> Those dusty high-roads of the aimless dead
> Plaintive for earth; but rather turn and run

Brooke added that Gauguin grossly maligned the Tahitian ladies! The mood of the island lay heavy upon him after only a day or so there, and the moon was on the lagoon, and it was too warm for writing, he told Marsh. He would go and dream and float and woo nymphs.

Eddie Marsh wrote to tell him that *Georgian Poetry* had entered its ninth edition in triumph. About the same time, Brooke heard of the progress in the plan to publish a quarterly poetry periodical. The original intention had been to christen this *The Gallows Garland*, after Lascelles Abercrombie's Gloucester cottage home. But the organizers decided that this sounded too grim and might prove bad for business, so settled on the more innocuous title of *New Numbers*. The first of these quarterly garlands appeared in February 1914, with works by Abercrombie, Drinkwater, Gibson and Brooke. The remarkable thing about it was that although the quarterly was published from the remote hamlet of Ryton in Gloucestershire, and printed locally, too, it included *Not with Vain Tears* posted by Rupert from Tahiti only a month earlier! His other three contributions to this first number were *A Memory,One Day* and *Mutability*.

And as *New Numbers* came out, Brooke forwarded a further 'few things' as he put it. These comprised a priceless quartet: *The Great Lover*, *Retrospect*, *Hauntings*, and *Tiare Tahiti*. The former two he wrote in Mateia; *Hauntings* he composed while en route to Tahiti and finished off there; and *Tiare Tahiti* he wrote in its main town of Papeete.

After a week or so in Papeete, he withdrew some thirty miles along the coast to Mateia, which was a wonderful spot for working or lazing. Once more, Rupert sensed the overwhelming attraction of the Pacific surroundings, their fatalistic philosophy, perhaps purer and simpler than his complex civilization. At Mateia, he sat on a wide veranda, shaded from the sun, and overlooked a rich blue lagoon. Here he stretched out his legs and turned his mind to the good things of the earth elsewhere, as well as on Tahiti; and wrote

These I have loved:

Here he wrote the last four of his Canadian articles for the *Westminster Gazette*. And here he made love.

In Tahiti, everyone wore a white flower behind their ears, but it was whether the left or the right – or both – which was the important thing. Behind the right ear meant they were looking for a sweetheart; behind the left, they had found one; behind both, they were looking for a second!

Brooke saw the allure that the island must have had for Gauguin, who lived his last ten years there, a decade earlier. But as Brooke said, the artist's *Tahitians on the Beach* and other classics did not do justice to the exquisite colour and curve of the people.

Rupert realized only too well how, once settled there, the days and weeks would drift into months and years, till the will to return would be gone forever. But he was wise or restless enough not to grow tied to that extent, for he knew in his heart he regretted the enlivening influence of Europe. Yet the dilemma was still sufficiently real, for he saw how much more honest was this tropic-sand life than the parade of pseudo-intelligentsia or the merely moribund encountered in England! It was only the thought of his real friends that swayed the scales.

In February he completed *Tiare Tahiti*. In it, he seemed still clearly under the Pacific influence, but this could not be wholly bad if it were capable of stimulating such idyllic images. Once more it reveals the curious complex. If he believed the beauty he found at Tahiti, why did he want to leave? Probably only because he would always want to move on from any place after as long as he had spent here. Three months on one island was a long time indeed. So the little land of Gauguin and Captain Bligh seeped into him. But he also contracted a form of coral-poisoning, intensified by bathing.

This illness proved the turning-point and brought home to him his vagabondage. He told Erica Cotterill all about his poisoned legs, and how he was being nursed by a girl 'with wonderful eyes'. In his passing depression, he admitted that he had lost a dream or two in trying to be a poet. Perhaps, he felt, he had been given some talent but not quite enough. He thought he had missed greatness, and also let the world slip by him. He had seen fish and skies the colour of a rainbow; waves breaking in glistening line on hot golden sand; a radiant brown girl on a green and purple reef. What was left? What could come after the scarlet dawns, the cooling winds? England was two worlds away: from the Pacific to America, then across the Atlantic.

As April came alike to Tahiti and Grantchester, Rupert sailed from the surrender of the islands, back to San Francisco. *Partir, c'est toujours mourir en peu.* He felt this acutely as he leaned over the rail and followed the wake of the ship straight back to the bay, and his eyes looked up and beyond the green coast and Papeete to the jutting peaks of the hills, ringed in clouds. How wonderful these people were, and how much they meant to him. He told them he would return. He wanted to. But would he?

Chapter Eleven

Back to 'imprisoning civilization'

San Francisco rose all around the bay, like an arm waiting to imprison him. Brooke hated its houses and public conveyances and worst of all – collars! For a few days, he stayed with the former friends of Berkeley University, and then he realized that although he might look healthy, he was also wild and woolly! After eleven months on the move, his clothes had frayed, and he had little money left. All he got for the *Westminster Gazette* articles was four guineas per piece.

So he decided it was time to head east again. Leaving California he actually went south-east to take in the Grand Canyon and the rugged wastes of Arizona.

High on a plateau with a coat to protect him against spring snow, Rupert sat and stared away in the distance, then down at the mile-deep drop inside the canyon. For six or seven miles on each side, the great cliffs of rock rose stark, primeval. But unlike his soul, he thought, it had peace in it. The wind whipped the snow into a whirl of whiteness, suddenly blotting out the whole scene; and he stepped down from this vastness, back into a world of surprising culture, for he met friends of the serious theatre in Chicago, of all places.

Rupert registered at the Auditorium Hotel, and then, as he had been thinking more about the theatre on the journey home, he scribbled a note to Maurice Browne, whom Harold Munro had said was a moving force in the experimental drama of America. Browne was running the Chicago Little Theatre, which had its headquarters next door to Brooke's hotel, in the Fine Arts Building. Brooke and Browne had been chasing each other for two years before this day in the third week of April, when they finally met.

Browne read the note on his arrival at the theatre and at once telephoned asking Brooke to come round and meet them all. In a couple of minutes, Rupert was waltzing down the sidewalk and hurried into the neighbouring building. Browne's mother-in-law threw her arms around his neck; Brooke promptly kissed Browne's wife; and five minutes later the four of them were marching arm in arm down Michigan Avenue for a drink of beer.

Brooke had no idea that Chicago was so culturally advanced, although he did know of Harriet Monroe's magazine *Poetry*. All the arts flourished in this exciting era of the mid-west, and Ben Hecht was one of the producers trying out ideas in the Little Theatre during these years.

Maurice Browne had been born and educated in England but came out to the United States to start this ardent, almost amateur group. Their talent was very professional, though, for their whole lives were revolving and wrapped around that courageous Little Theatre. To Brooke, they were people of his very own, and he extended his original itinerary of only three or four days in Chicago, which he had imagined as hellish, to ten.

This week and a half merged itself into an endless, riotous blur of all-night talks, club sandwiches, and then the dawn, chill-clean over Lake Michigan. Rupert was entranced with the theatre and rhapsodized over it, then suddenly he would be withdrawn for a while. Yet speaking or silent, he spent practically his whole ten days there while they were rehearsing.

Browne himself was an actor as well as producer, and his wife played the leading roles as Ellen Van Volkenburg. After the day's rehearsing, they returned to their studio, a few blocks south overlooking the lake, and here Brooke showed them all his South Seas treasures. He presented Ellen with several delicate chains made of Pacific shells.

'Why, they're beautiful, Rupert' she cried excitedly, fastening them around her neck as she rushed over to look in the property mirror on the wall. He also gave her a copy of Hilaire Belloc's *Four Men* which he seemed to know almost by heart! Then the three of them sat up night after night talking, singing folk-songs, reading poetry, creating their own world in a setting of one chair, a table, and some packing cases; they did not have much money. This was what Rupert had missed, and now he really wondered why he had been so hesitant to leave the Islands.

On three successive mornings, they saw the sun inching up, a misty flame sphere on the still lake. Then they went to bed for a few hours and at the 11 a.m. breakfasts, Ellen found both men quite adult and cross, in contrast to the imagery they had been weaving. But back at the theatre the magic returned.

One special night, Maurice lured into the studio group an Iowa poet and attorney, Arthur Davison Ficke. The bait which Browne offered was 'poetry, beer and Brooke'. Ficke bit it firmly, for like Browne he had already read Rupert's *Poems*. So started one of those memorable nights of declamation, discussion, disagreement – on free verse, rhyming, writing for the theatre, and anything else. Ficke came, saw, and fell under the incomparable Brooke personality, and celebrated the event in a sonnet, *Portrait of Rupert Brooke*.

They persuaded Rupert to read his poems to them, almost all he had written, including *Lithuania* and the copies of the South Seas works. It was midnight by now as he sat on the floor of the studio, with his knees hunched up, his arms hugging them, and his back propped against the wardrobe.

He blushed with unaffected pleasure at any comment on especial loveliness. The group sat as statues, Ficke in the decrepit rocker, and the others sprawled over odd pieces of furniture. Rupert read with his usual mellifluence, the soft slight stress of rhythm and rhyme, and his tones touched each one of them as they heard this flow of lyric verse from a voice in the night. And as Rupert reached *Tiare Tahiti*, all Chicago seemed asleep and the room suspended in space and time, an island oasis in the ocean of the poem.

The days fled. Maurice was so impressed with *Lithuania* that he wanted to produce it when he could. But both he and Ellen were due to visit England, and the idea had to be postponed. According to their arrangements, they were due to sail a week after Brooke, but Rupert had the marvellous idea of accompanying them, so set about planning it. Meanwhile, he continued his Chicago stay, and his long legs strode freely down the sidewalks. In his right hand, he swung a broad-brimmed, high-crowned, featherweight hat, which was plaited from South Seas straw, and so a precious possession. Every woman, and every other man, stopped in the street to look round at this bronzed radiant figure. The wind blew the Chicago dust and cinders through his hair, but he did not mind. He was in his own world again.

Rupert went to Washington during the first week of May, with the intention of meeting his Lady of the Chateau. On 10 May he wrote to Browne from the capital asking if he could travel over on the same boat as them. Browne told him they would be sailing on the *Philadelphia* from New York on the 29th, but Brooke did not get this immediately as he was now in New Jersey en route for 'Bawston' having fled from Pittsburgh in terror! Finally he fixed a berth on the *Philadelphia*.

Once in Boston, he hurried over to Harvard for a return visit to the university and met a guest lecturer there from England for the summer term. This proved to be Bertrand Russell, his brilliant friend from the days of Cambridge and the Apostles. Here in newer Cambridge, the two met again with the campus at its spring best. Brooke was in top form, and Russell remembers his handsome and bronzed features specially well.

Earl Russell told me how Rupert arrived wearing his South Seas hat, and a certain Professor Perry wondered who on earth was the strange young man. Brooke started to expound in fun the theory that the South Seas had lapsed into a state of decadence ever since cannibalism had ceased there, twenty or so years earlier! As he proceeded, Perry became more and more shocked, not realizing that it was all humorous, and afterwards turned to Russell saying: 'I don't think he should talk about cannibalism at all – let alone speak in favour of it!' Perry did not know, of course, that this was Rupert's favourite funny topic in his correspondence home from the Pacific, nor that he had written a sonnet on it as well, opening on this momentous note:

> The limbs that erstwhile charmed your sight
> Are now a savage's delight;

One of Bertrand Russell's pupils at Harvard that term was T.S. Eliot, who heard his whole course of lectures. There is no record of any meeting between Brooke and Eliot, although it is quite possible.

Brooke got to New York the week before sailing date and stayed at the Hotel McAlpin, Greeley Square. Here he received a set of portraits taken by the Chicago photographer, Eugene Hutchinson. Unfortunately, a middle-aged lady's pictures had been forwarded to Rupert in error for his own, but an exchange of letters remedied this.

So 29 May dawned and he met the Brownes under the shadow of the ship. Ellen Van Volkenburg said that Rupert Brooke was looking very fit and Rupertish, and was carrying his straw hat, an overcoat, Hutchinson's photographs, some magazines, books and a writing case. His arrival on board caused a succès de scandale!

Tucked away on deck, Rupert found Ellen with a pen in hand. . .

'Are you writing to your mother? May I add a line at the end please?'

He scrawled his own message on hers: Ave atque vale.

Then the ship left the majesty of Manhattan a year to the day after the SS *Cedric* had arrived there, bringing Brooke on his travels. He felt much more than a year older; still young in heart, but beyond his twenty-six years.

The trio settled down to enjoy a week aboard the liner and then a June homecoming at Plymouth. The voyage went well. After dinner on the first full day out, they played three-handed bridge and then strolled round the deck in the sea starlight. Next day, they saw for the tenth time a small podgy girl whom Brooke had christened playfully 'the pig child'. Ellen wondered what he would have called her in childhood days.

Their steward could never quite remember what people had ordered for meals, and always seemed to be bringing extra ice-cream, which Rupert, with a martyred air and the look of a wicked baby, consumed with extra layers of rhubarb and sugar!

The three of them continued the game of naming suitably the more outrageous people on board. Two sisters about twenty and twenty-two, who had their eyes on every man in sight, Rupert adorned as Mimi and Fifi.

Ellen recorded that Brooke was having signs and eyes cast at him, and even a married woman took a snapshot of him because – as she said – he had such a noble head. Two tables down from their own, a young girl gazed at him dumbfounded and 'beautifully melancholy'.

Just after the halfway mark, they met a painter, Ronald

Hargreave, and on 3 June spent most of the day in his cabin working on his idea for projecting scenery on to the backdrop of a stage by painting a miniature landscape on glass and putting it in a camera. Brooke had heard of this theory before, and was keen to explore its possibilities.

Next day, he and Ellen installed themselves in their accustomed corner facing the stern of the ship. The white wake foamed and creamed away into the distance, and the breeze blew fresh. Rupert was in wonderful form, recounting stories of the great and near-great for three hours. As he finished one, he set his eyes astern until that peculiar little cast came into one of them, then he ran his fingers through his hair with ferocious energy, paused, grasped his nose, tweaked it gently, pulled his blanket high around his head leaving none for his legs, and launched into the next tale!

Later on, the three men decided to write sonnets, and settled into a businesslike attitude to do so. Hargreave achieved one or two but threw them overboard in disgust! Brooked dashed off a pretentious pair entitled *The True Beautitude* and *Plato was Right*. Then later still in the library, to the inspiration of beer and lemonade, Maurice, Rupert and Ellen composed a ballad, each writing alternate lines. This started symbolically:

Sing not of California, no

Now they were a mere twenty-four hours out of Plymouth, where they were due to berth about 6.30 p.m. The day ended triumphantly with a marconigram from Eddie Marsh inviting them all to dine with him in his rooms. The Brownes had other commitments, but they were at least actually in touch with England.

Land's End and the Lizard loomed and faded as 5 June dragged by. In the afternoon, Ellen joined Brooke at the taffrail, and found him sniffing ecstatically the scent of new-mown hay from the fields near the east Cornwall cliffs. Together they watched the mellow brown and green landscape take shape, and once more Rupert told her that he still loved Cathleen Nesbitt, and would see her as soon as he could.

As the two of them were leaning over the rail looking down at the water, they suddenly heard a noise behind them. They turned their heads sharply and a camera clicked to an apologetic smile.

133

Then a woman came up and asked in an embarrassed way who they were. They, also rather embarrassed, answered 'Brooke-Browne' whereupon she volunteered that she was enquiring for the friend who had taken the photograph and simply had to know, as they looked quite the most interesting people on board and would not talk to anyone else, and seemed to have such a good time. They assured her that they were the most interesting – and did have a good time!

Rupert found out that the Russian Ballet was on in London, so the Brownes decided to defer a projected Paris trip for a while. They had plans to operate an English theatre in the French capital.

So the *Philadelphia* docked on time and they saw Rupert off on the London train, arranging to meet the following week. While Brooke had been abroad, he had visualized the route the train would follow, and he dozed content to know that it was steaming through the West Country night, past Teignmouth, with its connections with Keats, and Exeter, and on across Wiltshire.

Finally he stirred, to see the shape of Paddington curving into view at the dead of night. He leapt out of the carriage, trotted down the platform still carrying his hat, and at 2.45 a.m. on the morning of 6 June, was met by wild shrieks from Eddie Marsh, Denis Browne and Cathleen Nesbitt. He flung his arms around Cathleen. He was home.

Chapter Twelve

Home to England and the War

Eight wild weeks followed. After only a few hours' sleep, Rupert rushed on to Rugby.

'Must pay my respects to the Ranee,' he told them.

He got home the same afternoon, of Saturday 6 June, and assured his mother that all was well.

'I can only stay two or three days now' he admitted, 'because Eddie Marsh has booked seats for the Russian Ballet on Thursday with Maurice Browne and Ellen – the two I met in Chicago.

Mrs Brooke was not really surprised. She had got beyond that by now. She contented herself just knowing that he was alive and happy, realizing her world and his seemed planets apart. Rupert wrote to tell the Brownes about Thursday and arranged to meet them as they were comparative strangers to London.

The night of 11 June was to be yet another of those immortal times. Brooke came up from the smoke of Rugby; the Brownes got to Town promptly, too and they all dined out with Eddie Marsh and Cathleen before going on to the ballet. Marsh had been lucky to get tickets, which were almost unobtainable anywhere, so the five of them appreciated it all the more. Almost as soon as they sat down, they saw some of the legendary London figures who were there as well; Arnold Bennett, Queen Alexandra, and the Bernard Shaws.

But it was the ballet which was all-important. The moment when the conductor's baton flicked up, and the lights went down. The magic moment of expectant silence. Then the music sounded and the first of the two ballets of the evening began; *Les Papillons* and then *Petrouchka*. Fokine had given way as choreographer to the fabulous Nijinski. Rupert gazed at the scene spellbound by its beauty. This was life. Now he really felt back among the living and civilization again. The Russian Ballet and his old and new friends. He glanced sideways to reassure himself. Yes, this was really Cathleen beside him. Her provocative profile darkly silhouetted in the reflection from the footlights. And Eddie, dear Eddie, with Maurice and Ellen on the other side. This was how it would be, always, he thought. He'd been a fool to be away for so long, exiled on those islands. Always? Or just for the few weeks till August. Here, he was at his zenith, more mature, yet still with his delightful humour, gentleness, modesty. Rupert sat there entranced, as the butterflies spread their wings, and then the tragic beauty of Petrouchka, the sad-face clown puppet, and his hopeless love for Ballerina. Rupert saw some parallel to his own life, but tonight he really felt too jolly for tears. The evening passed in a flash of feet, colour, movement, music, and suddenly they were outside Covent Garden, walking along Floral Street in the fresh, fragrant June air. But the night had not yet begun: this night that they would all remember.

'Come on back to Raymond Buildings' Eddie invited them.

About 11.15 p.m., as well as the ballet party, a whole host of other friends descended on the rooms in Gray's Inn to welcome Rupert back from his wanderings. It was a surprise planned by Eddie Marsh. Norman Wilkinson, Alfred Rothenstein, Granville Barker with his wife Lillah McCarthy, Henry Ainley, Harold Monro, Wilfrid Gibson, Basil Dean, and others! Fiesta flared into life as midnight chimed across the Inn. The noise grew to a tumult of élan.

Here was a cross-section of poetry, painting and the theatre to open their arms again to Brooke. And through the scene like a dream moved the exquisite Cathleen Nesbitt: too intelligent an actress to be merely a star. The Brownes found it all dreamlike, too, especially the chilling nectar of iced coffee produced at the psychological second by Marsh's master cook!

In one night, Brooke took up practically every string he had dropped a year before. He talked animatedly, passionately, to everyone, especially Basil Dean. And among the guests tirelessly flitted the figure of Eddie himself, his high-pitched voice and bird-like manner covering keen pleasure at having mustered all these brilliant people under one roof; his own.

Back to Basil Dean, who had come to act in London from Liverpool. Marsh had liked Dean's performance and got in touch with him through Galsworthy. Dean was then doing *The Silver Box* and soon found himself drawn into that charmed circle of Eddie's, through whom he met Gordon Bottomley, Ivor Novello, then in the extreme youth of his promise, and now Brooke. Marsh had become the paterfamilias of this entire group of young artists seeking release from the complacent materialism of the recent Edwardian era.

Yes, things were certainly stirring on the Georgian scene. Dean had married only in April and had been touring Italy as a honeymoon. Marsh heard, and so invited the two of them to this reunion for Rupert. And at once Dean and Brooke agreed with each other from that first moment. Brooke, still looking deeply bronzed, and strangely like some Greek god that night.

They sat on the stone stairs outside the main room – there was scarcely anywhere else to go – and talked in excited, staccato tones of the new drama they both sought so much. Dean yearned for his castle in the air, a new theatre devoted to the worthwhile dramatic art. But he had neither the money nor the access to it – only a fierce faith and obstinate hope. Inspired by the achievements of the Moscow Arts Theatre, Dean had long talked of such a place for London, where the new poets and poetic dramatists could be heard. Brooke took up this theme vehemently, too, fired by examples of the new spirit in painting all around them jostling for place with the established eighteenth century. Everything seemed to be too damned established. If it weren't the eighteenth it was the nineteenth century. Classic art or bourgeois reaction. Even the Edwardian seemed no better. It was all too safe. Everything cut and dried. The standards set. God, how he hated convention, Rupert thought. Yet the world was good, too. Look at these wonderful people. After all, it was an exciting year to be alive – and a fateful one. An exciting, enthralling, engrossing evening, too; each moment of it, vivid, vital.

Rupert had his clear-eyed look of enchantment about him. To

137

Dean, he was freer in attitude and outlook than even their contemporaries, a modern, born half a century ahead of his time.

Here he was, in the small hours of the morning of Friday, 12 June, 1914, Brooke beginning to sketch the plot for a play he had carried in his mind half across the world to this stone staircase in Gray's Inn. Brooke epitomizing what was the best in the traditional and the new. Diaghilev was setting the town in a whirl; Leon Bakst threw conventional colourists into a frenzy of dismay using blue with green for the first time; and Rupert Brooke embodying it all; this fresh impetus in the arts. For he was of the theatre, painting and poetry: he was part of Flecker's 'Hassan' and the post-impressionist painters. He was young 1914.

And he was still living poetry. The final scene of this eventful night came when he solemnly danced to a Polynesian sway with a certain Jane, who had red hair and mouth, over the mown grass of Gray's Inn at dawn!

Nothing happened early on Friday! But in the evening, the Brownes and Marsh and Brooke met Lascelles Abercrombie for dinner at Simpsons. Rupert had not met him before, though familiar with his work and often quoting it. The man himself was small and shy, with spectacles and straight hair; he appeared wearing a peculiar little green hat which tipped up in front.

On Saturday, Brooke and the Brownes had lunch with the Granville Barkers, but Rupert, for once outshone, crumbled his bread in a slightly jealous silence throughout the meal! So he was human after all. Perhaps the adulation this week had turned his head a little; perhaps not.

Later, he brightened up, as they picked up Gibson and Monro after an early evening snack, and headed for the ballet again – this time queueing for seats in the gallery. Thronging the pit or gallery of the Garden and Drury Lane at this time were the leading young writers and painters, men later world famed. They all seemed part of the general new movement, and used to boast in fun that the most important audiences of the London season were seen in the gallery. Packed like 'ecstatic sardines' – Basil Dean's phrase! – they would rush out at the intervals to talk to friends, or greet them across the uncomfortable, curved gallery.

So it was, on this Saturday night. Then back inevitably to Eddie Marsh's and a mosaic of music, conversation, colour and dance.

Brooke, Abercrombie, Monro and Gibson talked metaphysics at each other, and Browne, the entire night. The erudite Abercrombie emerged best, but eventually Sunday dawned and the time came for bed.

Next day, Ellen and Maurice visited the Gilbert Murrays, whose hopes for Rupert's future loomed great, while Brooke himself was arranging to take Abercrombie, Gibson and Drinkwater to a quiet place in his mother's new car to discuss the August *New Numbers*. But this projected meeting never occurred, as Mrs Brooke demanded the car on some 'nefarious political business', Rupert wrote. Meanwhile, that issue of *New Numbers* went to press with some of Rupert's best poems: *Tiare Tahiti, Retrospect, The Great Lover, Waikiki* and *Hauntings*.

Maurice and Ellen postponed leaving London for the Continent for twenty-four hours to enable Brooke to join them in London on Thursday 18 June for a final evening together. With Rupert and Cathleen the bond between them, they dined and talked far into another day. Just before they all parted, they stretched their arms across the table and clinked glasses to the future, and the future of drama. Rupert's glass to Ellen, Maurice's to Cathleen.

Invitations showered on Brooke, one to a garden party which the Prime Minister held in July. He was asked to it through the usual channels of Eddie Marsh. Cathleen and Denis Browne were also invited. Brooke was determined to enter it in his extra-large South Seas hat, but his courage dwindled as he espied the array of top hats, formal dress, and splash of navy and khaki uniforms. Just in time it dawned on him that it was all very well being unconventional among his own kind, but he could not merge into the crusty society gathering as he was – so he did not go.

'I'll wait for you round at Charing Cross Station' Rupert called to them as he loped off!

They left before the end of the party and strolled round to the station to discover him, as arranged, hunched moodily on a seat there nibbling at strawberries, and still truculently wearing his hat!

July continued the merry-go-round of plays, debates, midnight suppers; Rupert was trying to make up for time lost abroad by fitting in as many events as each day allowed. On 5 July, for instance, he wrote one of his typical notes to Hugh Dalton, whom he had not seen since returning from the South Seas:

139

Dear Hugh,

I find I can't get back in time for Tuesday night. I'm sorry. I am free as the wind on Thursday night. Are you? You can shelve your wife. Nothing shall occupy me on Thursday night till I hear from you. Write immediately to Rugby. All other times I am dining with E. Gosse, or H. James, or S. Olivier, and others of my contemporaries. How horrible it is to be a bachelor.

The meeting was sealed, and Rupert picked up Dalton at his chambers in the Temple. They dined alone together and Brooke recounted all his adventures. The two men – still young – faced each other and smiled as they remembered the years before Brooke's voyagings. Those times when they were young in years. Now they were almost twenty-seven. But their young-in-heart outlook on life would never desert them, never change.

Brooke was the same Rupert that Dalton had known at King's, though more assured now. Yet despite his assurance, their old eternal questions stayed unsolved. Perhaps because of this searching they would never lose their zest, however long or short their span. 'He made poetry of his questionings, and spared neither himself, nor love, nor the beloved.' So said someone of Rupert Brooke. And here he was, in July 1914, still a ferment of feeling, with all the impulses of man pounding in him.

During July he returned to Cambridge for a day or two, and dined with Arthur Benson, who noticed a maturer person since the travels.

Brooke had actually asked himself to dinner, much to Benson's pleasure, and he talked freely of his three months with a native chief in Tahiti, and many other things. Benson sounded him out about his willingness to do some teaching at Cambridge, and Brooke responded readily, though admitting that he had no intention of making teaching his life. Brooke did not talk about himself to Benson, except in reply to direct questions. When he discussed the South Seas, it was more with the place than the person of Brooke. But Rupert joined most of the talk with relish, even if he did not reveal any startling sentiments. In America, he told Benson, he had found himself merely a receptive organism, although he had managed to grind out a few ramshackle articles.

The evening together passed easily, amicably, and Rupert idled through the twilit streets, seeing again with a pang the silhouettes of the colleges and churches, exactly as they had always been and as they would remain. This was as much at home as he could ever be. Still he looked to Grantchester as a haven, and gave it as his permanent address always. The Old Vicarage. Perhaps he felt he would be remembered best by it.

A lunch meeting this time, with John Drinkwater, in Soho, at a colourful little restaurant near Golden Square, just far enough away from the bustle of Regent Street. Elsewhere, another bustle seemed to be growing louder; Europe looked threatening. Brooke talked to Drinkwater quite eagerly about the possibility of his helping Quiller-Couch in English at Cambridge next term. But through it all, Drinkwater detected a note of foreboding and disbelief. A sense that Rupert knew even as he was saying this, that he would not be teaching at the University, nor seeing Grantchester. It was a tone which later crystallized into the calm acceptance that touched all his deeds after August.

By the end of July, he regarded war as inevitable, and went to stay with his mother from 31 July till 3 August. At first, he was deeply anxious that it should be avoided if possible, and then gradually convinced that the country had no alternative but to do its duty.

On 2 August, he wrote to Eddie Marsh saying that he would be going to stay with the Cornfords in Norfolk for a week or so. At that stage, he had the idea of becoming a war correspondent or agricultural worker in France if he could not fight. He asked Marsh to let him know of any job possible, but at the Admiralty Eddie had his hands very full during the first days of August. Rupert ended by observing that he would be twenty-seven the next day; he had enjoyed July very much, though it was now only a lovely vision.

'Do you have a Brussels-before-Waterloo feeling' he ended, 'that we'll all – or some – meet with other eyes in 1915? . . .

He came down to London on his birthday and was in a musichall watching faded meaningless acts when a screen was suddenly thrust on stage and a flickering film projector announced to the audience. WAR DECLARED WITH AUSTRIA. Brooke trooped out into the streets, where stunned crowds were gathering around Trafalgar Square. Special midnight editions of the newspapers were already arriving, and as he watched the people about him, he was close to tears.

Next day, he made various futile efforts to get into something, and then decided to accept the invitation to visit the Cornfords in Norfolk after all. Here he had time to think what to do. Mrs Brooke wrote that 'he hated the idea of fighting, his love of humanity was so great and his desire to benefit it so deep'. But amid the calm, flat East Anglian landscape, his mind cleared too. He thought of days in Germany – now the enemy – and an April morning on the lake south of Berlin. And a Munich night with students who had sung, smoked and drank from 8 till 1. These things he would see no more. Nor would the Russian Ballet return. He thought of the words 'England' and 'Germany' and 'England' seemed to flash like a line of foam. Grey, uneven little fields, and small ancient hedges rushed before him, wild flowers, elms and beeches, gentleness. . . At one moment, he was in an Atlantic liner, sick for home, making Plymouth at nightfall. And then at last he muttered to himself:

'Well, if Armageddon's on, I suppose one should be there.'

He didn't know whether he was glad or sad. It was a new feeling.

On 10 August, he returned home to tell his mother that he must fight. And a week after war had been declared, he came back to London. The decision was deep, but once made, never doubted.

Chapter Thirteen

Royal Naval Division at Antwerp

In the stuffy summer heat from 11 to 24 August, Brooke tore over all parts of London trying to get into something useful, and for a day or two even did drill in the faint hope of joining a corps as a private. But after what seemed an interminable time, he was offered a commission by Winston Churchill in the newly formed Royal Naval Division. He and Denis Browne both joined the Anson Battalion in late September.

Some groups of the Royal Naval Volunteer Reserve were not needed afloat with the Fleet, so camps had been formed at Deal during August for shore service. These were the nucleus of what was known as the Royal Naval Division. The two brigades had their camps at Walmer and Betteshanger Park respectively, the latter lent by Lord Northbourne. And it was to the Anson Battalion of the Second Naval Brigade that Rupert and Denis were commissioned. Eddie Marsh saw them off at Charing Cross Station early one Saturday morning for Betteshanger, looking very smart in their brand new uniforms. Less than two months before, at this same station, Rupert had been munching his strawberries disconsolately while the Premier's garden party took its conventional course!

Betteshanger Park looked beautiful in the turning foliage of early autumn, and far from the nightmare of war which was nearer than they imagined. Four battalions – Hood, Howe, Nelson and Anson – comprised the Second Brigade, and Brooke's battalion was under the distinguished command of Colonel Cornwallis-West.

During the remaining days of September, they carried out sham fights and night attacks, together with musketry training over at Chatham. His letters home to Mrs Brooke were full of the life which was so strange and new. Some of it he liked very much, the companionship and foolishness and fun; other parts irked him, though he managed to laugh these off. Taking it altogether, he was remarkably happy and began to feel that by compulsion, a purpose had entered his life. And he rested content to let it lead him where it would. It was all out of his hands now.

Part of this abbreviated course, occupying only a week or two, was route marching. Rupert led his platoon along the Kentish country lanes singing such ditties as 'Hello, Hello, who's your lady friend?' and 'Sing a song of Bonnie Scotland' and the inevitable 'Tipperary'. He looked as if he was loving every minute of it, and while they were marching at ease, he gazed around at the rugged hills encircling Betteshanger, as if inscribing them on his memory. Here was his England seen from a new angle and at a strange time. Different dimensions now.

Sunday, 5 October, 5 a.m. Over the before-dawn air, a bugle blew and the voice of the brigade major shouted:

'Officers, get up immediately. We are leaving for France today.' Breakfast was at 7 a.m. The Second Brigade started to march to Dover about two hours later. Rupert was in front of his platoon, with their packs on their backs, as they crunched the weary miles down to Dover pier. More songs passed the journey, and Brooke joined in them all: 'There's a man selling beer over there'; 'Wash me in the water'; 'One man went to mow', which occupied more than a mile, and many more. They paused at midday for a snack and then plodded on right through the afternoon till the defiant lines of Dover Castle heaved on to the skyline and they dropped downhill to the town and quay. When the officers finally got all the men and baggage on board their ship, they found that everyone had forgotten to provide an evening meal for the commissioned men. So a sortie into the town was made, which produced roast beef washed down with lemonade and cider; and then all was ready for sailing.

About 9.30 p.m., just as the people of Dover were thinking of their beds, the ship eased away from the pier and nosed towards the Channel and France. Searchlights were trained on her, as Rupert lay down on an upper deck and dozed, with a greatcoat for cover. The sea again, but no sound of gentle surf or palms beside the beach.

By 4 a.m. on Monday morning, the ship had anchored off Dunkirk, where it lay hove-to for eight endless hours, with the sea too rough to enter harbour. This must have been the worst possible treatment for all on board, and they uttered a prayer of relief at noon when the ship finally managed to drag herself into Dunkirk.

Before the train took them towards Belgium, which they were supposed to be helping to save, Cornwallis-West addressed them and concluded with the words: 'Remember you are British'.

Dawn came as the train drew into Ghent with rain hammering hard on the carriage windows. Rupert remembered other train trips. Yet here he did not know his destination. It was 5.45 a.m., they were cold and hungry – but still somehow cheerful. A short step and then on towards the war. A strange sensation, being conveyed right to the front by mainline train. Now it was 9 a.m. on the 6th, and the first signs of war met the train. Away ahead, shrapnel was bursting around Antwerp, and two captive balloons suspended in the sky directed German fire to the Belgian forces.

As the train steamed on, Brooke saw with a sense of tragedy hundreds of Belgians building trenches against the enemy advance.

The Germans had been in a struggle with the Belgian army on 28 September, and commenced a big bombardment of the outer line of defensive forts around Antwerp. The Belgian guns of mere 4 and 6-inch calibre were pitiful when opposed to 12, 16 and 17-inch howitzers. It would clearly only be a matter of time. The Marine Brigade of the Royal Naval Division had been rushed into the defence on 3 October, and the First and Second Brigades had been due on the 5th. But now it was the 6th, and the situation grew hourly more desperate. Belgium was being ravaged – and savaged. The hope was to gain delaying time to enable the Belgian army to retire more or less intact to a line behind Ghent, where they could join the main British and French forces.

The Belgians welcomed the Royal Naval Division, but it really arrived too late. Their train got to Antwerp about 10 p.m. and they were at once handed jugs of light beer which slopped over the top and ran down the outside. Girls rushed up to embrace the officers as they lined up to lead the troops. One flung herself on Rupert

145

with flags and kisses, and others handed apples and chocolates to the men.

Cries of 'Vivent les Anglais' and 'Heep! Heep!' sounded over the din of cannonades exploding only a few miles from the city. Brooke and Denis Browne led their little platoons through Antwerp and the outskirts till they were four miles from the station. After a meal, another five miles to Vieux-Dieu. Here Brooke saw hundreds of Belgian troops resting after days of ordeal. He wondered what would happen next, but did not mind now, for he felt the wound to Belgium as if it were his own. At Vieux-Dieu, they halted, and heard that they would be going up to the firing line soon. They heard, too, the bass boom of the guns, nearer now. No peace. The wounded came in all the time on stretchers, and a horse was brought back from the front literally riddled with bullets.

The afternoon passed and they were quartered for a few hours in an old deserted château. The sailors bivouacked in the garden, while the officers occupied the house itself. An ironic moment. From somewhere in its depths, a servant still there cooked them a meal of veal, bread and black coffee, which they ate at dusk by the light of a candle thrust in the neck of an empty wine bottle. The windows were plastered in brown paper for blackout, and the distinguished group consumed the food like gourmets, but with their pocket knives or fingers! As the candle flickered, its light fell on the faces of Cornwallis-West, Arthur Asquith, son of the Prime Minister, Denis Browne and Rupert. They drained their coffee from broken tumblers or milk jugs, and all the time the guns boomed in the background, shaking the window-frames and the brown paper. At nine o' clock the candle burned low, and its grease traced white streaks down the bottle; they rested quietly.

Five hours later, a Belgian officer stumbled into the darkened room and awoke the colonel. The time had come to move up to the front. Slightly dazed, they got up and dressed and went into the garden to the men. The fortress troops and the Second Belgian Division – all exhausted almost beyond endurance – and the three brigades of the Royal Naval Division were to hold the Germans at bay. The prospect seemed farfetched. In fact, the whole operation savoured of the unreal as they made a romantic march through the night to Fort No.7. Every so often, they passed a sentry, and finally they reached their spot at dawn. Rupert could not remember the date, but it did not matter. A year ago to the day, he had been heading south-west towards Honolulu, now he was here before Antwerp, facing thousands of Germans. And next year?

The trenches they had to occupy would not be much use, they understood. It would probably be bayonets. As the day of the 7th lightened, all their eyes turned to the River Nethe. The forts fired away spasmodically. They saw trenches at the end of a turnip field. The day passed without direct action. A hospital had been rigged up in a bomb-proof dugout, and stretchers were supplemented by blinds torn from a nearby villa. Then only a matter of hours after they had left it, shells smashed the château where they had sheltered during the night.

Now another night fell, pitch and cold, with a bitter wind blowing over the front. Suddenly an alarm. They started to fire into the inky blackness. Searchlights stabbed the night. Shells began to burst.

'Enemy approaching barbed wire' someone yelled, but it was only a reconnaissance from across the river. The fighting got no nearer.

A surprise attack killed seven Belgian gunners in the fort close to them, but the Naval Division had hardly any casualties. The Marines had the worst of the fighting. But although it did not reach Rupert's brigade, there was no rest for them and by the 8th they were pretty exhausted, though still with some cheery spirits among them. Breakfast consisted of one biscuit, a piece of bread, a small slice of cheese, and a mug of coffee.

As another day cleared, the shells got worse and they could see Antwerp deluged, a burning city. The Germans had got nearer in the night, and intermittent shrapnel peppered down all along the front. Despite this desperate situation, a lunch of steak was served at exactly teatime!

And as they ate, with their rifles and bayonets at the ready in case of need, the fate of the city had long since been settled. It all fitted in with the unreality of these Antwerp days.

Suddenly the drum-major said: 'We'll have to clear out, sir, we're almost cut off on all sides. They mean to throw their heavy guns on us tonight.'

He had prophesied correctly. Within an hour, orders came from headquarters for them to evacuate quickly. Soon after, their trenches were pulverized. They reached Scheldt. Nearby, Belgians had set fire to their own petroleum tanks at Hoboken, to stop the Germans getting them. The fuel blazed brilliantly, and its fumes proved too powerful for some of the sailors. Burning oil flooded one field and horses and cattle lay frizzled in a second.

Rupert looked back at the smoke in the sky – the scorching city of Antwerp – and at some of the 100,000 refugees staggering with a few pitiful possessions. He swallowed hard. Then the fumes from the fuel blurred his eyes and he turned away.

'Now through' he shouted, as the smoke and flame thinned for a second. 'Keep your heads and run through it.'

They got through the fire, to a hundred yards of safety. Then they were exposed to a mile or more of enemy crossfire. At last they crossed the river and the worst was passed.

But not all the whole Division had to march against time to escape. They overtook thousands more refugees next day, who cast hopeless glances back at their doomed city. Then, at last, they got a train to Bruges. Denis Browne was suffering from sore feet by now, not really surprising. He was able to rest them a brief while at the Hotel Majestic in Ostend, before they sailed for England on Sunday 11 October. Exactly a week had gone since the Brigades set out. Seven days inscribed on their hearts as a mixture of frustration, folly, but most of all, sheer tragedy at the fall of Belgium.

Fog stopped them outside Dover, and it was not until Monday evening that they regained a footing on the good earth of Kent, surprised to see it again at all. They had not had their clothes off since the start, and slept on the ground with no covering or else on the deck of the ship. Rupert was quiet that night as he lay thinking of those seven days.

After it was all over, Churchill wrote:

The naval brigades bore themselves admirably under the artillery fire of the enemy. The Belgian people will never forget that the men of the Royal Navy and Royal Marines were with them in their darkest hour of misery.

Towards the end of October, Brooke wrote to Maurice Browne, now back in America, telling him of Antwerp and the Germans' guilt. It was clear that the smoke in the sky over the Belgian city was still smouldering in his brain and that he would not erase it. He was home for further training and asked Maurice if there was any chance of borrowing a pair of field glasses to replace those he had lost in Belgium. Although Browne could not afford to buy any, by a minor miracle, he happened to meet a Countess Capponi who had some Zeiss which she forwarded to Rupert.

Rupert told him, too, of 'the other Nesbitt' being in the artillery and that he himself was still with Denis Browne and F.S. Kelly, a professional pianist who had won the Diamond Sculls before the war.

November passed with a number of irritating re-groupings among the various battalions, but by December Brooke and his officer friends were once more all together again in the Hood battalion. Now they found themselves no longer in Kent but at Blandford Camp on the Dorset Downs. It was a healthy, bracing place, but rather wild in winter and, of course, muddy. They wallowed from hut to hut and across the neighbouring countryside, but at least each officer had his own coke stove for comfort at the end of the day!

The camp was run on rigid naval lines, with watches kept and liberty men 'going ashore'. This last touch, however, was not altogether inappropriate by the time they had ploughed through liquid mud to civilization. Each battalion had its own flagstaff and vied to have the best lines. In fact, the camp was quite a self-contained town of wooden huts, institute, YMCA, and even a cinema.

Brooke was glad to renew his knowledge of the Dorset Downs, and whenever he could, looked southward and remembered Lulworth and the past which already seemed several lives away. But he had little time for contemplation, as the daily routine of drill, dress, boots, and food, had to be organized for his platoon.

Nevertheless, as he lay in his hut at night, he began sketching the form of a group of sonnets which he wanted to reflect the mood of the men he met and saw about him. The rain beat against the timber walls, but he was unaware. And then, before he drowsed off in his sleeping-bag, he thought of the future and marriage. He wanted to have a child before anything happened to him. But by now he had decided that he was not meant to marry. There it rested. 'It'll end in my muddling that' he wrote.

Cathleen Nesbitt was rehearsing J.M. Synge's '*Deidre of the*

Sorrows' for a short run at the Little Theatre. She and Rupert had resumed their love affair, conducted for a year by post and cable. They saw several ballets at Drury Lane before Cathleen was due to embark on a tour in a rather 'dreary drama'. By this time, Rupert was at Blandford Camp and wrote to tell her that he could get leave on a particular Sunday. Where would she be on tour? The answer was Great Yarmouth. He was tickled about the name of the theatre where she was playing – The Aquarium!

Rupert made a 'hideous journey' from Blandford to reach the fishing port in the late afternoon. They had supper of fresh bloaters, which they found ambrosial. Cathleen recalled that Rupert sat on the floor 'before the green-flamed driftwood fire, and put his head in my lap and said, "Read to me something beautiful".' She chose John Donne. Rupert said to her: 'Donne is aways the best. He knows about love and death. . .' Cathleen and Rupert scarcely saw each other again, though they exchanged love letters.

Christmas came. He was not due for leave till afterwards, so he spent the holiday keeping an eye on drunken sailors who insisted on dancing involved movements in their shoeless feet. The food was fair, but Rupert decided it needed augmenting, so sent a telegram to a friend begging for mince-pies and cakes for sixty men! A strange Christmas, with the crisp air outside and the spark of warmth within from human hearts. Rupert relaxed for a day or two and pondered on this Dorset hillside. In the precise place of the huts was once an Iberian fort against the Celts; a Celtish one against the Romans; Roman one versus Saxons. Here was England, its eternal earth beneath his boots. And here were its men, inarticulate but true. So were born the five war sonnets, as 1914 ended.

Brooke was second watch for leave, so when the first half returned glumly to Blandford, he was making arrangements for a dinner party in London. On New Year's Eve, he proposed to Marsh that they should choose either the Carlton Grillroom or Cafe Royal. The vote went for the Carlton, where they were joined by Arthur Asquith and Violet, later Lady Bonham-Carter. This was Brooke's treat to them, as he had just been awarded compensation by the Admiralty for the loss of some manuscripts on the Antwerp expedition.

The night recaptured for a few hours the magic of the previous summer, but with a difference. England was slowly waking, Rupert observed, and it was rather a wonderful sight. The new spirit spread through all of them, and in fact their feelings were worlds away from the old days. Brooke told them of his menial duties as Sub Lieutenant, RNVR, and they toasted the young year, about to be born.

James Elroy Flecker died at Davos at the end of 1914 and Rupert wrote an obituary in *The Times*. 'His muse was stertorous with the lush slumbers of the East.'

When this was printed, he was home at Rugby, spending the rest of his leave and finishing the five sonnets. He was also thinking more about religion. Too many people dismiss him as an absolute atheist, but his beliefs were less clear-cut. Certainly he could not convince himself of any immortality, but belief takes many forms. He had a boundless love of humanity and its potentialities for good. He had little love of material things. These alone mean more than many people's observances. 'I think he groped, like most of us, in the regions of the spirit' said Lady Violet Bonham-Carter. And the splendour of the sonnets were the result.

By mid-January the sonnets were completed, and as they were wanted for the current *New Numbers*, he posted them straight off to Gloucestershire. The proofs reached him as he stayed at Canford Manor, near the camp, with influenza, and within forty-eight hours he had written to Maurice Browne, asking him to send copies of the sonnets enclosed to Harriet Monroe, editor of *Poetry* in America.

'I wrote,' he said, 'under pressure of military labours, some honest but too crude stuff for the N.N. (*New Numbers*) and I want to get gold for it from the Yanks, too.'

They gave him some sick leave to recuperate from the flu, and he came up to London at the end of January, staying with Eddie Marsh first and then at No. 10 Downing Street for a day or two with the Asquiths.

Then followed a final interlude before the Gallipoli affair.

As Rupert was allowed generous leave to recover completely, he decided to go down and see Wilfrid Gibson and the Abercrombies in Gloucester before returning to Blandford. And at once he walked back into a village of poetry and peace.

The full address of Lascelles Abercrombie and his wife was The Gallows, Ryton, Dymock, Gloucestershire, the house which had nearly named the *New Numbers*. Rupert saw its delicious black and white outline and stepped over the stone courtyard into a low-beamed room. Though the crimson ramblers were not in bloom, it still seemed as colourful and inviting as the first time he had been there just before the war.

He was not the first poet to visit the Abercrombies, for several went down there who had their youth in the golden days before 1914. There the earth is rich red loam, and the hillocks are covered with firs and birch. It was in the midst of the cider country, and acres of apple orchards unfolded. And in the spring, mile after mile of daffodils spilled over the ground.

Mrs Abercrombie met Brooke and for a minute her mind returned to his earlier visit and those other poets who had been there. John Drinkwater was very shy but very determined, and read some of his poems to them straight away, with a fashionable parson's voice and eyes on the ceiling! He turned up with a sleeping bag with the intention of sleeping under the great elms at the bottom of the garden, but on the first night asked to be let indoors as a horse kept blowing at him through the hedge!

The sight of Rupert Brooke brought back to her just how wonderful those days had been. She had a permanent tent under the 'seven sisters', as the elms were called, and she saw again her iron pot on the fire, with a duck and green peas stewing on the spring air. Then in summers past, she lay on a stoop of hay and watched the stars wander through the elms, listening as Lascelles, Drinkwater and Wilfrid Gibson sat around and recited their latest poems. She thought that she had found the wherefore of life, with a mind at rest.

Eddie Marsh, too, had been a frequent visitor, with his monocle fixed firmly in his aristocratic eye! He never minded the primitive house, although he was used to the comforts of London. Ivor Gurney was another poet Mrs Abercrombie remembered, seeing him first in khaki. Back at the front, an injury affected his mind; his subsequent verse was often spoilt by incoherence. The American, Robert Frost, received encouragement at The Gallows; W.H. Davies visited them just before the war and D.H. Lawrence, with the piercing blue eyes, they met in Italy.

And now Rupert Brooke stood there again, in the pale February sunlight, talking to the two young Abercrombie boys, David and Michael, four and two years.

The Gallows was a three-sided house based on the courtyard, and dated back about 300 years. Inside its black and white walls and thatch roof, ran one long room which led into a hall, library and little room. Upstairs were two bedrooms and a dressing room, while to get to the other two bedrooms it was necessary to descend again. The bathroom was a curtained-off recess by a huge chimneystack in the courtyard out of doors. And the bath – with cold water only – had to be filled from a long tube of red india-rubber stretched from a nearby pump! But what did that matter when they could climb a high hill and see a patchwork panorama of the wonderful West Country?

Mrs Abercrombie found Rupert as good-looking and glamorous as she had before, and with an added beauty of expression and radiance of youth. She saw his tawny colouring and eager eyes, and found him still friendly and high-spirited. But although Antwerp had happened three months earlier, he still seemed to reflect its mood and the recent flu. He was keen to throw himself into the thick of things and tried to tease Lascelles into joining him, but Abercrombie was not sufficiently fit.

Just before he left, they went outside, and Mrs Abercrombie stood beside him as he gazed at the garden and beyond. There in the summer, the huge sloping field, dropping down to the edge of the elms, had been ablaze with poppies scarlet in the sun – and Rupert had stood silently watching them. Now he looked at the field again and whispered:

'I shall remember that – always.'

Chapter Fourteen

If I should die . . .

On 25 February, King George reviewed the whole Naval Division with Winston Churchill accompanying him as First Lord of the Admiralty. Blandford looked bright on this fine, late-winter day, and the sun shone on swords and bayonets as they marched past the saluting base. Three cheers and the anthem ended the review. Now they knew they were bound for the Mediterranean. On the 27th, the last day in camp, they had friends and relations down to see them; many for the last time, with Gallipoli their grave. Violet Asquith said farewell to Brooke and Denis Browne. The same day, Rupert received via Eddie Marsh a pentagram charm to come back safely – given by a girl. He replied to Eddie saying: 'But what luck is, we'll all wait, and you'll see, perhaps'.

They left the camp at 7.15 the same evening, just after dark, wearing their new equipment with pith helmets, and carrying a pack. They marched to the small station of Shillingstone, the point to entrain, and were followed somewhat primitively by mules carrying the heavier baggage. After an hour or two of the waiting, which became inseparable from service life, the train finally heaved out about 3.30 the next morning, Sunday, 28 February for an unknown destination. They eased off their boots and slept through the rest of the night, to be jolted to consciousness in the 8 a.m. light of Avonmouth Docks, Bristol, where the *Grantully Castle* was waiting to sail in the early afternoon, convoyed by a couple of destroyers. The ship left the Bristol Channel behind by nightfall and reached the northern approaches to the Bay of Biscay next day, 1 March. She began to roll a lot as the waters of the Bay swelled, but the roughness passed, and by the following morning dolphins were sporting about near the vessel. A beautiful night heralded a calm day off Portugal and out of sight of land. In the evening, Denis Browne, F.S. Kelly, Henry Asquith and Brooke sang folk-songs on the sea air. Others in 'Winston's Wandering Wonders', as they were dubbed, included Sub Lieutenant Arthur Asquith, son of the Premier, Sub Lieutenant Campbell, son of Mrs Patrick Campbell and Lieutenant Bernard Freyburg. Freyburg and Sub Lieutenant Tisdall both won the VC. It was a brilliant officers' mess, full of wit and talent.

They were all excited at the prospect ahead. Mrs Brooke said that Rupert himself was exceedingly happy going out, commenting that if anyone could be said to be lucky in that way, they were.

Reflecting the fever of enthusiasm about this whole Constantinople expedition, Rupert wrote:

> It's too wonderful for belief. I had not imagined fate could be so kind. Will Hero's Tower crumble under the 15-inch guns? Will the sea be polyphloisbic and wine-dark and unvintage-able? Shall I loot mosaics from St. Sophia, and Turkish Delight and carpets? Should we be a turning point in History? Oh God! I've never been quite so happy in my life, I think. Never quite so pervasively happy: like a stream flowing entirely to one end. I suddenly realise that the ambition of my life has been – since I was two – to go on a military expedition against Constantinople.

And as he sailed outward, the *Sonnets* appeared in England, matching the mood, reflecting the feeling, of everyone in the country so exactly that they would soon be remembered by thousands. Just the right amount of sentiment went into them. For war was an emotional time, it brought men face to face with life and death.

In the evenings, when all became still, there was one officer usually pacing the deck alone. No-one thought of disturbing him, they knew by instinct that he wished to be alone. It was Rupert. He glowed in those quiet nights, drinking in their beauty after all the others had gone. He was only there through his love of England; the country he would never see again.

The ship reached the Straits of Gibraltar before dawn on 5 March, and after Divisions, at 9.30 each morning, they had a chance to see the Rock. On the following day, Brooke looked south this time, to the African coast and the white walls of Algiers nestling among the hills, with further off still, the snow-clad peaks of the mountains.

Patrick Shaw-Stewart came up to Brooke one afternoon and they chatted over books and people. Rupert told him how he was looking forward to reading Compton Mackenzie's next book. Mackenzie, who was to have his own memories of Gallipoli and later wrote that he had lived to hear Rupert Brooke sneered at for a romantic by the prematurely weaned young sucking pigs of the next generation.

They were north of Tunis on the 7th and put into Malta the next day, anchoring off Fish Quay. At mid-afternoon, the junior officers went ashore for supplies in the spring sunshine. The strong light cast colour over all Valetta, and Brooke noticed especially the head-dress of the women and the vividly green, shuttered houses. Then they dined at the Union Club and finished the day at a little water-front cafe, being rowed back to the ship over the moonlit water.

By noon next day, the island was receding as the *Grantully Castle* hurried eastward, past southern Greece to the blue-green Aegean, studded with superb islands. They reached Lemnos on the 11th, and anchored in Mudros Bay, where a series of wonderful sunsets lit the hills of Samothrace with a rich golden glow.

Brooke would watch motionless from the deck of the transport as the dusk deepened, darkened. And it occurred to him that the time had come to consider arrangements in case of his death. He wrote to Eddie Marsh making him his literary executor and requesting one or two simple wishes. Then he felt easier, and turned to a few fragments which he had been writing on the journey out. 'Golden phrases' he called them in fun. Much of this remained in his head only, but what was recorded revealed that Brooke had reached at last a mastery of poetry. But, like one of these very phrases, his future was fated to be an 'ungathered blossom'.

A week later, they received orders to sail into Turkish waters. This looked like the real assault, and an air of expectancy shivered through the ships moored in Mudros Bay. They sailed out on the morning tide and actually advanced some way beyond the entrance to the Dardanelles, but at that stage the orders were counter-manded and they were told to turn round and return to Lemnos. The whole thing had been a feint, much to the disgust of all.

Back at Lemnos, the rocky terrain made manoeuvres on land impracticable, and the men could not be cooped up indefinitely aboard ship. So when a request came for forces in Egypt, they were sent over to the flat expanses of that land on the 24th. Past the legendary isles of Patmos, Kos, Samos and Rhodes, the transport plodded in good weather, and reached Port Said three days later.

After disembarking just outside the docks area, they pitched tents on the sand, where they encountered a virus which resulted in effects rather similar to dysentery. After a five-day sortie towards El Kantara and back, followed by a visit to Cairo with Asquith and Shaw-Stewart, Rupert returned to camp with a temperature and a slightly swollen lip.

The Commander-in-Chief, Sir Ian Hamilton, reviewed the Royal Naval Division next day, with their arms flashing in the sun. But Brooke was ill in his tent, so Hamilton went to see him there, finding that despite his indisposition, Rupert still looked remark-ably handsome, and had quite a knightly presence stretched out on the sand. Hamilton did not want to risk any serious development from this illness, and in fact, would have preferred Brooke not to be going to Gallipoli, so he offered him a staff appointment at the base, one which would be useful but less dangerous. Rupert heard him in silence and thought about it, but after thanking Sir Ian, explained that having started this affair with his men, he must see it through – at least the first fight. Hamilton did what he could, however, by saying that the place would be kept open for him at any time, and had good reason to believe that Brooke would have accepted after the Dardanelles affair was over.

Meanwhile, he arranged for Rupert to be moved into more comfortable quarters in the Casino Palace Hotel, at Port Said, where the Naval Chaplain, Henry Foster, called to see him on 3 April. The attack of sunstroke, which it seemed to be, and the swollen lip left him a little dazed. Shaw-Stewart sat in the same room, also under the weather, while Foster chatted for some ten minutes to Brooke. Rupert pulled back the large mosquito net of white muslin hanging over his bed, and his eyes flashed brightly as he assured Foster that he would soon be better. The next day was

Easter Sunday, 4 April, when far across Europe in St Paul's Cathedral, the Dean, Dr Inge, quoted *The Soldier* – the last of the Sonnets – in his sermon.

The *Grantully Castle* was due out of Port Said on the 9th, for a rumoured landing on the Gulf of Saros. Brooke and Shaw-Stewart both said they felt fit for the campaign, but it proved to be another false alarm and the ship steamed back to the Greek Islands, to Scyros this time. A fancy-dress party helped to pass the days en route, and Rupert recovered enough to take part.

By the time they landed at Scyros on 17 April, he was apparently himself again, and started to explore this amazing island with its wild marbled mountains, glorious grape hyacinths, succulent langoustes, nightingales and goldfinches and the memories of Achilles and Theseus where never a ship now calls. . .

Rupert mingled with the mountain shepherds, whose dress had hardly changed since the heydays of Greece, and breathed the scent of sage and thyme, balsam and storax. Here was eternal spring, he felt, distilled into a single day.

After a Divisional Field Day on Tuesday, 20 April, spent travelling rough over the rugged ground in heavy heat, Rupert returned aboard and went to his cabin. Next morning he was clearly ill, and his lip again swollen seriously.

The ship swung to the tide in the roadstead of Trebouki. But only slightly, for the bay looked like a lake in the mild April day, and the light like a scarf about the peaceful hills.

Denis Browne received a cutting from *The Times* reporting Dean Inge's sermon and his praise for the sonnet. He read the paper softly to Rupert, who managed a slight smile. Then later on, they decided to transfer him to the French hospital ship lying nearby, *Duguay-Trouin*. He was moved by stretcher to a cutter and brought across.

His face was bloodless, but he gazed with large blue enquiring eyes. Arthur Asquith, tall and fair, came over with him to sit in the little white cabin of the round-house. Rupert was the only patient for this large staff, mobilized for possible casualties from the forthcoming Gallipoli campaign.

In the wireless room, messages began to arrive hourly. Sir Ian Hamilton was worried by the news which had been telegraphed to him, and Winston Churchill was also in touch. The only answer they could be given was that he grew weaker; worse. The surgeons struggled to neutralize the poison which seemed to have taken control. The tang of salt from the water, with balsam on the breeze, wafted into the cabin.

By the morning of 23 April, Rupert had become unconscious and they gave up hope. Asquith sat with him throughout the day, until 4.46 p.m. a voice whispered:

'England has lost her greatest poet.'

So Rupert Brooke died on the same date as Shakespeare and Wordsworth. St George's Day. The day of England.

> If I should die, think only this of me:
> That there's some corner of a foreign field
> That is for ever England. There shall be
> In that rich earth a richer dust concealed;

They placed his coffin in the poop and covered it with the flag. Sixteen palms lay beside it. The officers of the *Duguay-Trouin* laid on it a bunch of wild flowers, picked on Scyros and tied with the French colours. Arthur Asquith stood still, staring into the brief twilight.

They had already received sailing orders for the following morning, so the service could not be delayed, nor was there time to engrave a brass plate. Asquith called for a cauterizing iron and by a circle of lamps – a wreath of watchlights – he seared the simple words on the oak plank:

RUPERT BROOKE

The little procession of boats glided over the water like gigs. The night was soft, bestarred, with a sheen of moon. And the blended scents of the island drifted stronger and stronger as they neared the land. The boats steered for a little cove, as a pearl-white hue shimmered over the water.

The naval officers were waiting ashore, where they had put in earlier to find a worthy burial place. Beside these six were a dozen tall Australian soldiers, with broad-brimmed hats, as a guard of honour.

It was after nine when the funeral party started on its way up the gently sloping valley. Soon the course steepened, and it was hard to tell whether there had ever been any paths, for no trace remained. The ground was mainly marble, and the vegetation sparse; brushwood and little holly bushes, shadowy ghosts in the flickering lamplight. The lanterns lit only a few yards around and the petty officer bearers made slow headway. Sometimes they slipped or stumbled as the marble pebbles turned under their feet. Their boots trod down shrubs, and a mingling of musk and pepper rose as incense.

The wan moonlight lingered, and the flames from the torches trailed away in smoky tresses. No soul, no sound. The route became so unsure that men with lamps had to be posted every twenty yards to act as guides. It was nearly eleven when they at length reached the spot.

A perfect place, a mile up from the valley. Among an olive grove by a watercourse, dry then but torrential in winter. On either side, mountains flanked the ground, and Mount Khokilas was at its head. Over his head drooped an olive tree; around him, mauve-flowering sage.

They buried him by the cloudy moonlight. Asquith deepened the grave, and on the coffin were laid Rupert's helmet, belt and pistol – he had no sword. This could be his epitaph: he had no sword. A person of peace who went to war. They lined the grave with flowers and an olive wreath, and the chaplain read the simple service. Three volleys rang out round the mountains; the bugles sounded the *Last Post*. And then there was silence. Forever.

On his grave they heaped blocks of white marble, and at his head they planted a wooden cross. The six men who had dug the ground walked slowly down to the sea – Arthur Asquith, Patrick Shaw-Stewart, Denis Browne, Charles Lister, F S. Kelly and Bernard Freyburg.

In *The Times*, three days later, Winston Churchill wrote:

Rupert Brooke is dead. A telegram from the Admiral at Lemnos tells us that his life has closed at the moment when it seemed to have reached its springtime. A voice had become audible, a note had been struck, more true, more thrilling, more able to do justice to the nobility of our youth in arms engaged in this present war than any other – more able to express their thoughts of self-surrender, and with a power to carry comfort to those who watch them so intensely from afar. The voice has been swiftly stilled. Only the echoes and the memory remain; but they will linger.

During the last few months of his life, months of preparation in gallant comradeship and open air, the poet-soldier told with all the simple force of his genius the sorrow of youth about to die, and the sure triumphant consolations of a sincere and valiant spirit. He expected to die; he was willing to die for the dear England whose beauty and majesty he knew; and he advanced towards the brink in perfect serenity, with absolute conviction of the rightness of his country's cause and a heart devoid of hate for fellow-men.

The thoughts to which he gave expression in the very few incomparable war sonnets which he has left behind will be shared by the many thousands of young men moving resolutely and blithely forward into this, the hardest, the cruellest, and the least-rewarding of all the wars that men have fought. They are a whole history and revelation of Rupert Brooke himself. Joyous, fearless, versatile, deeply instructed, with classic symmetry of mind and body, ruled by high undoubting purpose, he was all that one could wish England's noblest sons to be in days when no sacrifice but the most precious is acceptable, and the most precious is that which is most freely proffered.

One day soon afterwards, Maurice Browne opened an envelope addressed to him in an unknown hand. And as he did so, the snapshot of Brooke, taken as the *Philadelphia* steamed into Plymouth Sound, dropped on to his desk. The accompanying letter from the woman said simply: If for a few days Youth walked among us, in its passing it left unnumbered years for memory of him who gave it so lavishly.

So Rupert Brooke died. But the legend lived and grew. A legend of a man and his work. But where does one end and the other start? How great was his poetry? Time has passed, time for the legend to fade and the worth of the work to be reviewed. Yet opinions still divide.

H.W. Garrod, formerly Professor of Poetry at Oxford, summed him up best of all:

It was when he got away from Cambridge that he began to be a great poet. For a great poet I do account him. He was also, beyond question, an interesting and rarely attractive young man, crowning vivid days with a death enviably romantic. But there are people who do not like this; who dislike mixing the poet and his poetry.

Garrod disagrees with them observing that a man's poetry is, after all, only one part of his greatness. Then he goes on:

He began to write really well in Munich. There for the first time you discover the real humour. There dies the charlatan. In the place of Swinburne now sits Stevenson. I wonder whether Stevenson had any effect on his visit to the South Seas? There he wrote 'Tiare Tahiti' and 'O haven without wave or tide', two poems I do not know how to praise enough.

He has in his most characteristic poetry an ingenuity unbeaten outside Marvell. It came to him from the metaphysical poets to whom – and Donne especially – he became more and more bound. Some of his effects I cannot easily match in the last 300 years. He has a large Elizabethan utterance.

Rupert Brooke has left us 25 poems of the first-rate. Yet the man himself is a fine addition to these . . .

The actual number of poems does not matter, nor which are thought best. That must always remain a question of personal preference. The vital thing is that although he died so young, Rupert Brooke has left us a living force of poetry, imperishable, inspired.

Part Two

Selected Poems

Second Best

Here in the dark, O heart;
Alone with the enduring Earth, and Night,
And Silence, and the warm strange smell of clover;
Clear-visioned, though it break you; far apart
From the dead best, the dear and old delight;
Throw down your dreams of immortality,
O faithful, O foolish lover!
Here's peace for you, and surety; here the one
Wisdom—the truth!—'All day the good glad sun
Showers love and labour on you, wine and song;
The greenwood laughs, the wind blows, all day long
Till night.' And night ends all things.
Then shall be
No lamp relumed in heaven, no voices crying,
Or changing lights, or dreams and forms that hover!
(And, heart, for all your sighing,
That gladness and those tears are over, over. . . .)

And has the truth brought no new hope at all,
Heart, that you're weeping yet for Paradise?
Do they still whisper, the old weary cries?
'Mid youth and song, feasting and carnival,
Through laughter, through the roses, as of old
Comes Death, on shadowy and relentless feet,
Death, unappeasable by prayer or gold;
Death is the end, the end!'
Proud, then, clear-eyed and laughing, go to greet
Death as a friend!

Exile of immortality, strongly wise,
Strain through the dark with undesirous eyes
To what may lie beyond it. Sets your star,
O heart, for ever! Yet, behind the night,
Waits for the great unborn, somewhere afar,
Some white tremendous daybreak. And the light,
Returning, shall give back the golden hours,
Ocean a windless level, Earth a lawn

165

Spacious and full of sunlit dancing-places,
And laughter, and music, and, among the flowers,
The gay child-hearts of men, and the child-faces,
O heart, in the great dawn!

1908

In Examination

Lo! from quiet skies
In through the window my Lord the Sun!
And my eyes
Were dazzled and drunk with the misty gold,
The golden glory that drowned and crowned me
Eddied and swayed through the room. . . Around me,
To left and to right,
Hunched figures and old,
Dull blear-eyed scribbling fools, grew fair,
Ringed round and haloed with holy light.
Flame lit on their hair,
And their burning eyes grew young and wise,
Each as a God, or King of kings,
White-robed and bright
(Still scribbling all);
And a full tumultuous murmur of wings
Grew through the hall;
And I knew the white undying Fire,
And, through open portals,
Gyre on gyre,
Archangels and angels, adoring, bowing,
And a Face unshaded. . . .
Till the light faded;
And they were but fools again, fools unknowing,
Still scribbling, blear-eyed and stolid immortals.

10 *November* 1908

Pine-Trees and The Sky: Evening

I'd watched the sorrow of the evening sky,
And smelt the sea, and earth, and the warm clover,
And heard the waves, and the seagull's mocking cry.

And in them all was only the old cry,
That song they always sing—'The best is over!
You may remember now, and think, and sigh,
O silly lover!'
And I was tired and sick that all was over,
And because I,
For all my thinking, never could recover
One moment of the good hours that were over.
And I was sorry and sick, and wished to die.

Then from the sad west turning wearily,
I saw the pines against the white north sky,
Very beautiful, and still, and bending over
Their sharp black heads against a quiet sky.
And there was peace in them; and I
Was happy, and forgot to play the lover,
And laughed, and did no longer wish to die;
Being glad of you, O pine-trees and the sky!

LULWORTH, 8 *July* 1907

167

Wagner

Creeps in half wanton, half asleep,
  One with a fat wide hairless face.
He likes love-music that is cheap;
  Likes women in a crowded place;
    And wants to hear the noise they're making.

His heavy eyelids droop half-over,
  Great pouches swing beneath his eyes.
He listens, thinks himself the lover,
  Heaves from his stomach wheezy sighs;
    He likes to feel his heart's a-breaking.

The music swells. His gross legs quiver.
  His little lips are bright with slime.
The music swells. The women shiver.
  And all the while, in perfect time,
    His pendulous stomach hangs a-shaking.

QUEEN'S HALL, 1908

Seaside

Swiftly out from the friendly lilt of the band,
    The crowd's good laughter, the loved eyes of men
    I am drawn nightward; I must turn again
Where, down beyond the low untrodden strand,
There curves and glimmers outward to the unknown
    The old unquiet ocean. All the shade
Is rife with magic and movement. I stray alone
    Here on the edge of silence, half afraid,

Waiting a sign. In the deep heart of me
The sullen waters swell towards the moon,
And all my tides set seaward.
                  From inland
Leaps a gay fragment of some mocking tune,
That tinkles and laughs and fades along the sand,
And dies between the seawall and the sea.

The Song of the Beasts
(Sung, on one night, in the cities, in the darkness)

Come awayl Come away!
Ye are sober and dull through the common day,
But now it is night!
It is shameful night, and God is asleep!
(Have you not felt the quick fires that creep
Through the hungry flesh, and the lust of delight,
And hot secrets of dreams that day cannot say?). . .
. . . The house is dumb;
The night calls out to you . . . Come, ah, come!
Down the dim stairs, through the creaking door,
Naked, crawling on hands and feet
—It is meet! it is meet!
Ye are men no longer, but less and more,
Beast and God . . . . Down the lampless street,
By little black ways, and secret places,
In darkness and mire,
Faint laughter around, and evil faces
By the star-glint seen—ah! follow with us!
For the darkness whispers a blind desire,
And the fingers of night are amorous . . . .
Keep close as we speed,
Though mad whispers woo you, and hot hands cling,
And the touch and the smell of bare flesh sting,
Soft flank by your flank, and side brushing side—
Tonight never heed!
Unswerving and silent follow with me,
Till the city ends sheer,
And the crook'd lanes open wide,
Out of the voices of night,
Beyond lust and fear,
To the level waters of moonlight,
To the level waters, quiet and clear,
To the black unresting plains of the calling sea.

1906

Dawn
(From the train between Bologna and Milan, second class)

Opposite me two Germans snore and sweat.
   Through sullen swirling gloom we jolt and roar.
We have been here for ever: even yet
   A dim watch tells two hours, two æons, more.
The windows are tight-shut and slimy-wet
   With a night's fœtor. There are two hours more;
Two hours to dawn and Milan; two hours yet.
   Opposite me two Germans sweat and snore . . . .

One of them wakes, and spits, and sleeps again.
   The darkness shivers. A wan light through the rain
Strikes on our faces, drawn and white. Somewhere
   A new day sprawls; and, inside, the foul air
Is chill, and damp, and fouler than before . . . .
   Opposite me two Germans sweat and snore.

The Call

Out of the nothingness of'sleep,
  The slow dreams of Eternity,
There was a thunder on the deep:
  I came, because you called to me.

            I broke the Night's primeval bars,
              I dared the old abysmal curse,
            And flashed through ranks of frightened stars
              Suddenly on the universe!

The eternal silences were broken;
  Hell became Heaven as I passed.—
What shall I give you as a token,
  A sign that we have met, at last?

            I'll break and forge the stars anew,
              Shatter the heavens with a song;
            Immortal in my love for you,
              Because I love you, very strong.

Your mouth shall mock the old and wise,
  Your laugh shall fill the world with flame,
I'll write upon the shrinking skies
  The scarlet splendour of your name,

            Till Heaven cracks, and Hell thereunder
              Dies in her ultimate made fire,
            And darkness falls, with scornful thunder,
              On dreams of men and men's desire.

Then only in the empty spaces,
  Death, walking very silently,
Shall fear the glory of our faces
  Through all the dark infinity.

            So, clothed about with perfect love,
              The eternal end shall find us one,
            Alone above the Night, above
              The dust of the dead gods, alone.

The Beginning

Some day I shall rise and leave my friends
And seek you again through the world's far ends,
You whom I found so fair,
(Touch of your hands and smell of your hair!),
My only god in the days that were.
My eager feet shall find you again,
Though the sullen years and the mark of pain
Have changed you wholly; for I shall know
(How could I forget having loved you so?),
In the sad half-light of evening,
The face that was all my sunrising.
So then at the ends of the earth I'll stand
And hold you fiercely by either hand,
And seeing your age and ashen hair
I'll curse the thing that once you were,
Because it is changed and pale and old
(Lips that were scarlet, hair that was gold!),
And I loved you before you were old and wise,
When the flame of youth was strong in your eyes,
    —And my heart is sick with memories.

1906

1908–1911

Sonnet

Oh! Death will find me, long before I tire
   Of watching you; and swing me suddenly
Into the shade and loneliness and mire
   Of the last land! There, waiting patiently,

One day, I think, I'll feel a cool wind blowing,
   See a slow light across the Stygian tide,
And hear the Dead about me stir, unknowing,
   And tremble. And I shall know that you have died,

And watch you, a broad-browed and smiling dream,
   Pass, light as ever, through the lightless host,
Quietly ponder, start, and sway, and gleam—
Most individual and bewildering ghost!—

And turn, and toss your brown delightful head
Amusedly, among the ancient Dead.

April 1909

Sonnet

I said I splendidly loved you; it's not true.
    Such long swift tides stir not a land-locked sea.
On gods or fools the high risk falls—on you—
    The clean clear bitter-sweet that's not for me.
Love soars from earth to ecstasies unwist.
    Love is flung Lucifer-like from Heaven to Hell.
But—there are wanderers in the middle mist,
    Who cry for shadows, clutch, and cannot tell
Whether they love at all, or, loving, whom:
    An old song's lady, a fool in fancy dress,
Or phantoms, or their own face on the gloom;
    For love of Love, or from heart's loneliness.
Pleasure's not theirs, nor pain. They doubt, and sigh
And do not love at all. Of these am I.

January 1910

Success

I think if you had loved me when I wanted;
    If I'd looked up one day, and seen your eyes,
And found my wild sick blasphemous prayer granted,
    And your brown face, that's full of pity and wise,
Flushed suddenly; the white godhead in new fear
    Intolerably so struggling, and so shamed;
Most holy and far, if you'd come all too near,
    If earth had seen Earth's lordliest wild limbs tamed,
Shaken, and trapped, and shivering, for *my* touch—
    Myself should I have slain? or that foul you?
But this the strange gods, who had given so much,
    To have seen and known you, this they might not do.
One last shame's spared me, one black word's unspoken;
    And I'm alone; and you have not awoken.

January 1910

Dust

When the white flame in us is gone,
   And we that lost the world's delight
Stiffen in darkness, left alone
   To crumble in our separate night;

When your swift hair is quiet in death,
   And through the lips corruption thrust
Has stilled the labour of my breath—
   When we are dust, when we are dustl—

Not dead, not undesirous yet,
   Still sentient, still unsatisfied,
We'll ride the air, and shine, and flit,
   Around the places where we died,

And dance as dust before the sun,
   And light of foot, and unconfined,
Hurry from road to road, and run
   About the errands of the wind.

And every mote, on earth or air,
   Will speed and gleam, down later days
And like a secret pilgrim fare
   By eager and invisible ways,

Nor ever rest, nor ever lie,
   Till, beyond thinking, out of view,
One mote of all the dust that's I
   Shall meet one atom that was you.

Then in some garden hushed from wind,
   Warm in a sunset's afterglow,
The lovers in the flowers will find
   A sweet and strange unquiet grow

Upon the peace; and, past desiring,
   So high a beauty in the air,
And such a light, and such a quiring,
   And such a radiant ecstasy there,

They'll know not if it's fire, or dew,
   Or out of earth, or in the height,
Singing, or flame, or scent, or hue,
   Or two that pass, in light, to light.

Out of the garden higher, higher. . . .
   But in that instant they shall learn
The shattering ecstasy of our fire,
   And the weak passionless hearts will burn

And faint in that amazing glow,
   Until the darkness close above;
And they will know—poor fools, they'll know!—
   One moment, what it is to love.

December 1909–*March* 1910

Kindliness

When love has changed to kindliness—
Oh, love, our hungry lips, that press
So tight that Time's an old god's dream
Nodding in heaven, and whisper stuff
Seven million years were not enough
To think on after, make it seem
Less than the breath of children playing,
A blasphemy scarce worth the saying,
A sorry jest, 'When love has grown
To kindliness—to kindliness!'. . .
And yet—the best that either's known
Will change, and wither, and be less,
At last, than comfort, or its own
Remembrance. And when some caress
Tendered in habit (once a flame
All heaven sang out to) wakes the shame
Unworded, in the steady eyes
We'll have,—*that* day, what shall we do?
Being so noble, kill the two
Who've reached their second-best? Being wise,
Break cleanly off, and get away,
Follow down other windier skies
New lures, alone? Or shall we stay,
Since this is all we've known, content
In the lean twilight of such day,
And not remember, not lament?
That time when all is over, and
Hand never flinches, brushing hand;
And blood lies quiet, for all you're near;
And it's but spoken words we hear,
Where trumpets sang; when the mere skies
Are stranger and nobler than your eyes;
And flesh is flesh, was flame before;
And infinite hungers leap no more
In the chance swaying of your dress;
And love has changed to kindliness.

The Fish

In a cool curving world he lies
And ripples with dark ecstasies.
The kind luxurious lapse and steal
Shapes all his universe to feel
And know and be; the clinging stream
Closes his memory, glooms his dream,
Who lips the roots o' the shore, and glides
Superb on unreturning tides.
Those silent waters weave for him
A fluctuant mutable world and dim,
Where wavering masses bulge and gape
Mysterious, and shape to shape
Dies momently through whorl and hollow,
And form and line and solid follow
Solid and line and form to dream
Fantastic down the eternal stream;
An obscure world, a shifting world,
Bulbous, or pulled to thin, or curled,
Or serpentine, or driving arrows,
Or serene slidings, or March narrows.
There slipping wave and shore are one,
And weed and mud. No ray of sun,
But glow to glow fades down the deep
(As dream to unknown dream in sleep);
Shaken translucency illumes
The hyaline of drifting glooms;
The strange soft-handed depth subdues
Drowned colour there, but black to hues,
As death to living, decomposes—
Red darkness of the heart of roses,
Blue brilliant from dead starless skies,
And gold that lies behind the eyes,
The unknown unnameable sightless white
That is the essential flame of night,
Lustreless purple, hooded green,
The myriad hues that lie between
Darkness and darkness! . . .
                                    And all's one
Gentle, embracing, quiet, dun,

179

The world he rests in, world he knows,
Perpetual curving. Only—grows
An eddy in that ordered falling,
A knowledge from the gloom, a calling
Weed in the wave, gleam in the mud—
The dark fire leaps along his blood;
Dateless and deathless, blind and still,
The intricate impulse works its will;
His woven world drops back; and he,
Sans providence, sans memory,
Unconscious and directly driven,
Fades to some dank sufficient heaven.

O world of lips, O world of laughter,
Where hope is fleet and thought flies after,
Of lights in the clear night, of cries
That drift along the wave and rise

Thin to the glittering stars above,
You know the hands, the eyes of love!
The strife of limbs, the sightless clinging,
The infinite distance, and the singing
Blown by the wind, a flame of sound,
The gleam, the flowers, and vast around
The horizon, and the heights above—
You know the sigh, the song of love!

But there the night is close, and there
Darkness is cold and strange and bare;
And the secret deeps are whisperless;
And rhythm is all deliciousness;
And joy is in the throbbing tide,
Whose intricate fingers beat and glide
In felt bewildering harmonies
Of trembling touch; and music is
The exquisite knocking of the blood.
Space is no more, under the mud;
His bliss is older than the sun.
Silent and straight the waters run.
The lights, the cries, the willows dim,
And the dark tide are one with him.

MUNICH, *March* 1911

180

The Hill

Breathless, we flung us on the windy hill,
   Laughed in the sun, and kissed the lovely grass.
   You said, 'Through glory and ecstasy we pass;
Wind, sun, and earth remain, the birds sing still,
When we are old, are old. . . .' 'And when we die
   All's over that is ours; and life burns on
Through other lovers, other lips,' said I,
   'Heart of my heart, our heaven is now, is won!'

'We are Earth's best, that learnt her lesson here.
   Life is our cry. We have kept the faith!' we said;
   'We shall go down with unreluctant tread
Rose-crowned into the darkness!' . . . . Proud we were,
And laughed, that had such brave true things to say.
—And then you suddenly cried, and turned away.

1910

The One Before the Last

I dreamt I was in love again
    With the One Before the Last,
And smiled to greet the pleasant pain
    Of that innocent young past.

But I jumped to feel how sharp had been
    The pain when it did live,
How the faded dreams of Nineteen-ten
    Were Hell in Nineteen-five.

The boy's woe was as keen and clear,
    The boy's love just as true,
And the One Before the Last, my dear,
    Hurt quite as much as you.

*   *   *

Sickly I pondered how the lover
    Wrongs the unanswering tomb,
And sentimentalizes over
    What earned a better doom.

Gently he tombs the poor dim last time,
    Strews pinkish dust above,
And sighs, 'The dear dead boyish pastime!
    But *this*—ah, God!—is Love!'

—Better oblivion hide dead true loves,
    Better the night enfold,
Than men, to eke the praise of new loves,
    Should lie about the old!

*   *   *

Oh! bitter thoughts I had in plenty.
    But here's the worst of it—
I shall forget, in Nineteen-twenty,
    You ever hurt a bit!

11 *January* 1910

The Life Beyond

He wakes, who never thought to wake again,
    Who held the end was Death. He opens eyes
Slowly, to one long livid oozing plain
    Closed down by the strange eyeless heavens. He lies;
    And waits; and once in timeless sick surmise
Through the dead air heaves up an unknown hand,
Like a dry branch. No life is in that land,
    Himself not lives, but is a thing that cries;
An unmeaning point upon the mud; a speck
    Of moveless horror; an Immortal One
Cleansed of the world, sentient and dead; a fly
    Fast-stuck in grey sweat on a corpse's neck.

I thought when love for you died, I should die.
It's dead. Alone, most strangely, I live on.

April–September 1910

Dead Men's Love

There was a damned successful Poet;
   There was a Woman like the Sun.
And they were dead. They did not know it.
   They did not know their time was done.
      They did not know his hymns
      Were silence; and her limbs,
      That had served Love so well,
      Dust, and a filthy smell.

And so one day, as ever of old,
   Hands out, they hurried, knee to knee;
On fire to cling and kiss and hold
   And, in the other's eyes, to see
      Each his own tiny face,
      And in that long embrace
      Feel lip and breast grow warm
      To breast and lip and arm.

So knee to knee they sped again,
   And laugh to laugh they ran, I'm told,
Across the streets of Hell . . .
                 And then
   They suddenly felt the wind blow cold,
      And knew, so closely pressed,
      Chill air on lip and breast,
      And, with a sick surprise,
      The emptiness of eyes.

MUNICH, 27 *February* 1911

184

Town and Country

Here, where love's stuff is body, arm and side
    Are stabbing-sweet 'gainst chair and lamp and wall
In every touch more intimate meanings hide;
    And flaming brains are the white heart of all.

Here, million pulses to one centre beat:
    Closed in by men's vast friendliness, alone,
Two can be drunk with solitude, and meet
    On the sheer point where sense with knowing's one.

Here the green-purple clanging royal night,
    And the straight lines and silent walls of town,
And roar, and glare, and dust, and myriad white
    Undying passers, pinnacle and crown

Intensest heavens between close-lying faces
    By the lamp's airless fierce ecstatic fire;
And we've found love in little hidden places,
    Under great shades, between the mist and mire.

Stay! though the woods are quiet, and you've heard
    Night creep along the hedges. Never go
Where tangled foliage shrouds the crying bird,
    And the remote winds sigh, and waters flow!

Lest—as our words fall dumb on windless noons,
    Or hearts grow hushed and solitary, beneath
Unheeding stars and unfamiliar moons,
    Or boughs bend over, close and quiet as death,—

Unconscious and unpassionate and still,
    Cloud-like we lean and stare as bright leaves stare,
And gradually along the stranger hill
    Our unwalled loves thin out on vacuous air,

And suddenly there's no meaning in our kiss,
    And your lit upward face grows, where we lie,
Lonelier and dreadfuller than sunlight is,
    And dumb and mad and eyeless like the sky.

Lust

How should I know? The enormous wheels of will
   Drove me cold-eyed on tired and sleepless feet.
Night was void arms and you a phantom still,
   And day your far light swaying down the street.
As never fool for love, I starved for you;
   My throat was dry and my eyes hot to see.
Your mouth so lying was most heaven in view,
   And your remembered smell most agony.

Love wakens love! I felt your hot wrist shiver,
   And suddenly the mad victory I planned
     Flashed real, in your burning bending head . . . .
My conqueror's blood was cool as a deep river
   In shadow; and my heart beneath your hand
     Quieter than a dead man on a bed.

Jealousy

When I see you, who were so wise and cool,
Gazing with silly sickness on that fool
You've given your love to, your adoring hands
Touch his so intimately that each understands,
I know, most hidden things; and when I know
Your holiest dreams yield to the stupid bow
Of his red lips, and that the empty grace
Of those strong legs and arms, that rosy face,
Has beaten your heart to such a flame of love,
That you have given him every touch and move,
Wrinkle and secret of you, all your life,
—Oh! then I know I'm waiting, lover-wife,
For the great time when love is at a close,
And all its fruit's to watch the thickening nose
And sweaty neck and dulling face and eye,
That are yours, and you, most surely, till you die!
Day after day you'll sit with him and note
The greasier tie, the dingy wrinkling coat;
As prettiness turns to pomp, and strength to fat.
And love, love, love to habit!
                              And after that,
When all that's fine in man is at an end,
And you, that loved young life and clean, must tend
A foul sick fumbling dribbling body and old,
When his rare lips hang flabby and can't hold
Slobber, and you're enduring that worst thing,
Senility's queasy furtive love-making,
And searching those dear eyes for human meaning,
Propping the bald and helpless head, and cleaning
A scrap that life's flung by, and love's forgotten,—
Then you'll be tired; and passion dead and rotten;
And he'll be dirty, dirty!
                              O lithe and free
And lightfoot, that the poor heart cries to see,
That's how I'll see your man and you!—
                                         But you
—Oh, when *that* time comes, you'll be dirty too!

187

Blue evening

My restless blood now lies a-quiver,
  Knowing that always, exquisitely,
This April twilight on the river
  Stirs anguish in the heart of me.

For the fast world in that rare glimmer
  Puts on the witchery of a dream,
The straight grey buildings, richly dimmer,
  The fiery windows, and the stream

With willows leaning quietly over,
  The still ecstatic fading skies . . .
And all these, like a waiting lover,
  Murmur and gleam, lift lustrous eyes,

Drift close to me, and sideways bending
  Whisper delicious words.
                                    But I
Stretch terrible hands, uncomprehending,
  Shaken with love; and laugh; and cry.

My agony made the willows quiver;
  I heard the knocking of my heart
Die loudly down the windless river,
  I heard the pale skies fall apart,

And the shrill stars' unmeaning laughter,
  And my voice with the vocal trees
Weeping. And Hatred followed after,
  Shrilling madly down the breeze.

In peace from the wild heart of clamour,
  A flower in moonlight, she was there,
Was rippling down white ways of glamour
  Quietly laid on wave and air.

Her passing left no leaf a-quiver.
    Pale flowers wreathed her white, white brows.
Her feet were silence on the river;
    And 'Hush!' she said, between the boughs,

May 1909

The Charm

In darkness the loud sea makes moan;
And earth is shaken, and all evils creep
About her ways.
              Oh, now to know you sleep!
Out of the whirling blinding moil, alone,
Out of the slow grim fight,
One thought to wing—to you, asleep,
In some cool room that's open to the night,
Lying half-forward, breathing quietly,
One white hand on the white
Unrumpled sheet, and the ever-moving hair
Quiet and still at length! . . .

Your magic and your beauty and your strength,
Like hills at noon or sunlight on a tree,
Sleeping prevail in earth and air.

In the sweet gloom above the brown and white
Night benedictions hover; and the winds of night
Move gently round the room, and watch you there,
And through the dreadful hours
The trees and waters and the hills have kept
The sacred vigil while you slept,
And lay a way of dew and flowers
Where your feet, your morning feet, shall tread.

And still the darkness ebbs about your bed.
Quiet, and strange, and loving-kind, you sleep.
And holy joy about the earth is shed;
And holiness upon the deep.

8 November 1909

Finding

From the candles and dumb shadows,
    And the house where love had died,
I stole to the vast moonlight
    And the whispering life outside.
But I found no lips of comfort,
    No home in the moon's light
(I, little and lone and frightened
    In the unfriendly night),
And no meaning in the voices . . . .
    Far over the lands, and through
The dark, beyond the ocean,
    I willed to think of *you*!
For I knew, had you been with me
    I'd have known the words of night,
Found peace of heart, gone gladly
    In comfort of that light.

Oh! the wind with soft beguiling
    Would have stolen my thought away
And the night, subtly smiling,
    Came by the silver way;
And the moon came down and danced to me,
    And her robe was white and flying;
And trees bent their heads to me
    Mysteriously crying;
And dead voices wept around me;
    And dead soft fingers thrilled;
And the little gods whispered . . .
                                    But ever
    Desperately I willed;
Till all grew soft and far
    And silent. . .
                    And suddenly
I found you white and radiant,
    Sleeping quietly,
Far out through the tides of darkness,
    And I there in that great light

190

Was alone no more, nor fearful;
   For there, in the homely night,
Was no thought else that mattered,
   And nothing else was true,
But the white fire of moonlight,
   And a white dream of you.

1909

Song

'Oh! Love,' they said, 'is King of Kings,
   And Triumph is his crown.
Earth fades in flame before his wings,
   And Sun and Moon bow down.'—
But that, I knew, would never do;
   And Heaven is all too high.
So whenever I meet a Queen, I said,
   I will not catch her eye.

'Oh! Love,' they said, and 'Love,' they said,
   'The gift of Love is this;
A crown of thorns about thy head,
   And vinegar to thy kiss!'—
But Tragedy is not for me;
   And I'm content to be gay.
So whenever I spied a Tragic Lady,
   I went another way.

And so I never feared to see,
   You wander down the street,
Or come across the fields to me
   On ordinary feet.
For what they'd never told me of,
   And what I never knew;
It was that all the time, my love,
   Love would be merely you.

The Voice

Safe in the magic of my woods
   I lay, and watched the dying light.
Faint in the pale high solitudes,
   And washed with rain and veiled by night,

Silver and blue and green were showing.
   And the dark woods grew darker still;
And birds were hushed; and peace was growing;
   And quietness crept up the hill;

And no wind was blowing. . .

And I knew
That this was the hour of knowing,
And the night and the woods and you
Were one together, and I should find
Soon in the silence the hidden key
Of all that had hurt and puzzled me—
Why you were you, and the night was kind,
And the woods were part of the heart of me.

And there I waited breathlessly,
Alone; and slowly the holy three,
The three that I loved, together grew
One, in the hour of knowing,
Night, and the woods, and you—-

And suddenly
There was an uproar in my woods,
The noise of a fool in mock distress,
Crashing and laughing and blindly going,
Of ignorant feet and a swishing dress,
And a Voice profaning the solitudes.

The spell was broken, the key denied me,
And at length your flat clear voice beside me
Mouthed cheerful clear flat platitudes.

You came and quacked beside me in the wood.
You said, 'The view from here is very good!'
You said, 'It's nice to be alone a bit!'
And, 'How the days arc drawing out!' you said.
You said, 'The sunset's pretty, isn't it?'

*   *   *

By God! I wish—I wish that you were dead!

April 1909

Dining-Room Tea

When you were there, and you, and you,
Happiness crowned the night; I too,
Laughing and looking, one of all,
I watched the quivering lamplight fall
On plate and flowers and pouring tea
And cup and cloth; and they and we
Flung all the dancing moments by
With jest and glitter. Lip and eye
Flashed on the glory, shone and cried,
Improvident, unmemoried;
And fitfully and like a flame
The light of laughter went and came.
Proud in their careless transience moved
The changing faces that I loved.

Till suddenly, and otherwhence,
I looked upon your innocence.
For lifted clear and still and strange
From the dark woven flow of change
Under a vast and starless sky
I saw the immortal moment lie.
One instant I, an instant, knew
As God knows all. And it and you
I, above Time, oh, blind! could see
In witless immortality.
I saw the marble cup; the tea,
Hung on the air, an amber stream;
I saw the fire's unglittering gleam,

The painted flame, the frozen smoke.
No more the flooding lamplight broke
On flying eyes and lips and hair;
But lay, but slept unbroken there,
On stiller flesh, and body breathless,
And lips and laughter stayed and deathless,
And words on which no silence grew.
Light was more alive than you.

194

For suddenly, and otherwhence,
I looked on your magnificence.
I saw the stillness and the light,
And you, august, immortal, white,
Holy and strange; and every glint
Posture and jest and thought and tint
Freed from the mask of transiency,
Triumphant in eternity,
Immote, immortal.

              Dazed at length
Human eyes grew, mortal strength
Wearied; and Time began to creep.
Change closed about me like a sleep.
Light glinted on the eyes I loved.
The cup was filled. The bodies moved.
The drifting petal came to ground.
The laughter chimed its perfect round.
The broken syllable was ended.
And I, so certain and so friended,

How could I cloud, or how distress,
The heaven of your unconsciousness?
Or shake at Time's sufficient spell,
Stammering of lights unutterable?
The eternal holiness of you,
The timeless end, you never knew,
The peace that lay, the light that shone.
You never knew that I had gone
A million miles away, and stayed
A million years. The laughter played
Unbroken round me; and the jest
Flashed on. And we that knew the best
Down wonderful hours grew happier yet.
I sang at heart, and talked, and eat,
And lived from laugh to laugh, I too,
When you were there, and you, and you.

A Channel Passage

The damned ship lurched and slithered. Quiet and quick
   My cold gorge rose; the long sea rolled; I knew
I must think hard of something, or be sick;
   And could think hard of only one thing—*you*!
You, you alone could hold my fancy ever!
   And with you memories come, sharp pain, and dole.
Now there's a choice—heartache or tortured liver!
   A sea-sick body, or a you-sick soul!

Do I forget you? Retchings twist and tie me,
   Old meat, good meals, brown gobbets, up I throw.
Do I remember? Acrid return and slimy,
   The sobs and slobber of a last year's woe.
And still the sick ship rolls. 'Tis hard, I tell ye,
To choose 'twixt love and nausea, heart and belly.

December 1909

Victory

All night the ways of Heaven were desolate,
　　Long roads across a gleaming empty sky.
　　Outcast and doomed and driven, you and I,
Alone, serene beyond all love or hate,
Terror or triumph, were content to wait,
　　We, silent and all-knowing. Suddenly
　　Swept through the heaven low-crouching from on high,
One horseman, downward to the earth's low gate.

Oh, perfect from the ultimate height of living,
　　Lightly we turned, through wet woods blossom-hung,
Into the open. Down the supernal roads,
　　With plumes a-tossing, purple flags far flung,
Rank upon rank, unbridled, unforgiving,
Thundered the black battalions of the Gods.

Day and Night

Through my heart's palace Thoughts unnumbered throng;
　　And there, most quiet and, as a child, most wise,
High-throned you sit, and gracious. All day long
　　Great Hopes gold-armoured, jester Fantasies,
　　And pilgrim Dreams, and little beggar Sighs,
Bow to your benediction, go their way
　　And the grave jewelled courtier Memories
Worship and love and tend you, all the day.

But, when I sleep, and all my thoughts go straying,
　　When the high session of the day is ended,
And darkness comes; then, with the waning light,
　　By lilied maidens on your way attended,
Proud from the wonted throne, superbly swaying,
　　You, like a queen, pass out into the night.

197

The Old Vicarage, Grantchester
(Café des Westens, Berlin, May 1912)

Just now the lilac is in bloom,
All before my little room;
And in my flower-beds, I think,
Smile the carnation and the pink;
And down the borders, well I know,
The poppy and the pansy blow . . .
Oh! there the chestnuts, summer through,
Beside the river make for you
A tunnel of green gloom, and sleep
Deeply above; and green and deep
The stream mysterious glides beneath,
Green as a dream and deep as death.
—Oh, damn! I know it! and I know
How the May fields all golden show,
And when the day is young and sweet,
Gild gloriously the bare feet
That run to bathe . . .
                              Du lieber Gott!

Here am I, sweating, sick, and hot,
And there the shadowed waters fresh
Lean up to embrace the naked flesh.
Temperamentvoll German Jews
Drink beer around;—and *there* the dews
Are soft beneath a morn of gold.
Here tulips bloom as they are told;
Unkempt about those hedges blows
An English unofficial rose;
And there the unregulated sun
Slopes down to rest when day is done,
And wakes a vague unpunctual star,
A slippered Hesper; and there are
Meads towards Haslingfield and Coton
Where *das Betreten's* not *verboten.*

εἴθε γενοίμην . . . would I were
In Grantchester, in Grantchester!—

Some, it may be, can get in touch
With Nature there, or Earth, or such.
And clever modern men have seen
A Faun a-peeping through the green,
And felt the Classics were not dead,
To glimpse a Naiad's reedy head,
Or hear the Goat-foot piping low: . . .
But these are things I do not know.
I only know that you may lie
Day-long and watch the Cambridge sky,
And, flower-lulled in sleepy grass,
Hear the cool lapse of hours pass,
Until the centuries blend and blur
In Grantchester, in Grantchester . . . .
Still in dawnlit water cool
His ghostly Lordship swims his pool,
And tries the strokes, essays the tricks,
Long learnt on Hellespont, or Styx.
Dan Chaucer hears his river still
Chatter beneath a phantom mill.
Tennyson notes, with studious eye,
How Cambridge waters hurry by. . .
And in that garden, black and white,
Creep whispers through the grass all night;
And spectral dance, before the dawn,
A hundred Vicars down the lawn;
Curates, long dust, will come and go
On lissom, clerical, printless toe;
And oft between the boughs is seen
The sly shade of a Rural Dean. . .
Till, at a shiver in the skies,
Vanishing with Satanic cries,
The prim ecclesiastic rout
Leaves but a startled sleeper-out,
Grey heavens, the first bird's drowsy calls,
The falling house that never falls.

God! I will pack, and take a train,
And get me to England once again!
For England's the one land, I know,
Where men with Splendid Hearts may go;
And Cambridgeshire, of all England,
The shire for Men who Understand;
And of *that* district I prefer

The lovely hamlet Grantchester.
For Cambridge people rarely smile,
Being urban, squat, and packed with guile;
And Royston men in the far South
Are black and fierce and strange of mouth;
At Over they fling oaths at one,
And worse than oaths at Trumpington,
And Ditton girls are mean and dirty,
And there's none in Harston under thirty,
And folks in Shelford and those parts
Have twisted lips and twisted hearts,
And Barton men make Cockney rhymes,
And Coton's full of nameless crimes,
And things are done you'd not believe
At Madingley, on Christmas Eve.
Strong men have run for miles and miles,
When one from Cherry Hinton smiles;
Strong men have blanched, and shot their wives,
Rather than send them to St. Ives;
Strong men have cried like babes, bydam,
To hear what happened at Babraham.
But Grantchester! ah, Grantchester!
There's peace and holy quiet there,
Great clouds along pacific skies,
And men and women with straight eyes,
Lithe children lovelier than a dream,
A bosky wood, a slumbrous stream,
And little kindly winds that creep
Round twilight corners, half asleep.
In Grantchester their skins are white;
They bathe by day, they bathe by night;
The women there do all they ought;
The men observe the Rules of Thought.
They love the Good; they worship Truth;
They laugh uproariously in youth;
(And when they get to feeling old,
They up and shoot themselves, I'm told). . .
    Ah God! to see the branches stir
Across the moon at Grantchester!
To smell the thrilling-sweet and rotten
Unforgettable, unforgotten
River-smell, and hear the breeze
Sobbing in the little trees.
Say, do the elm-clumps greatly stand

Still guardians of that holy land ?
The chestnuts shade, in reverend dream,
The yet unacademic stream?
Is dawn a secret shy and cold
Anadyomene, silver-gold?
And sunset still a golden sea
From Haslingfield to Madingley?
And after, ere the night is born,
Do hares come out about the corn?
Oh, is the water sweet and cool,
Gentle and brown, above the pool?
And laughs the immortal river still
Under the mill, under the mill?
Say, is there Beauty yet to find ?
And Certainty? and Quiet kind?
Deep meadows yet, for to forget
The lies, and truths, and pain? . . . oh! yet
Stands the Church clock at ten to three?
And is there honey still for tea?

Beauty and Beauty

When Beauty and Beauty meet
    All naked, fair to fair,
The earth is crying-sweet,
    And scattering-bright the air,
Eddying, dizzying, closing round,
    With soft and drunken laughter;
Veiling all that may befall
    After—after—

Where Beauty and Beauty met,
    Earth's still a-tremble there,
And winds are scented yet,
    And memory-soft the air,
Bosoming, folding glints of light,
    And shreds of shadowy laughter;
Not the tears that fill the years
    After—after—

1912

201

Song

All suddenly the wind comes soft,
    And Spring is here again;
And the hawthorn quickens with buds of green,
    And my heart with buds of pain.

My heart all Winter lay so numb,
    The earth so dead and frore,
That I never thought the Spring would come,
    Or my heart wake any more.

But Winter's broken and earth has woken,
    And the small birds cry again;
And the hawthorn hedge puts forth its buds,
    And my heart puts forth its pain.

1912

Unfortunate

Heart, you are restless as a paper scrap
    That's tossed down dusty pavements by the wind;
    Saying, 'She is most wise, patient and kind.
Between the small hands folded in her lap
Surely a shamed head may bow down at length,
    And find forgiveness where the shadows stir
About her lips, and wisdom in her strength,
    Peace in her peace. Come to her, come to her!'. . .

She will not care. She'll smile to see me come,
    So that I think all Heaven in flower to fold me.
    She'll give me all I ask, kiss me and hold me,
    And open wide upon that holy air
The gates of peace, and take my tiredness home,
    Kinder than God. But, heart, she will not care.

1912

The Busy Heart

Now that we've done our best and worst, and parted,
  I would fill my mind with thoughts that will not rend.
(O heart, I do not dare go empty-hearted)
  I'll think of Love in books, Love without end;
Women with child, content; and old men sleeping;
  And wet strong ploughlands, scarred for certain grain;
And babes that weep, and so forget their weeping;
  And the young heavens, forgetful after rain;
And evening hush, broken by homing wings;
  And Song's nobility, and Wisdom holy,
That live, we dead. I would think of a thousand things,
  Lovely and durable, and taste them slowly,
One after one, like tasting a sweet food.
  I have need to busy my heart with quietude.

1913

Love

Love is a breach in the walls, a broken gate,
  Where that comes in that shall not go again;
Love sells the proud heart's citadel to Fate.
  They have known shame, who love unloved. Even then
When two mouths, thirsty each for each, find slaking,
  And agony's forgot, and hushed the crying
Of credulous hearts, in heaven—such are but taking
  Their own poor dreams within their arms, and lying
Each in his lonely night, each with a ghost.
  Some share that night. But they know, love grows colder,
Grows false and dull, that was sweet lies at most.
  Astonishment is no more in hand or shoulder,
But darkens, and dies out from kiss to kiss.
  All this is love; and all love is but this.

1913

The Chilterns

Your hands, my dear, adorable,
  Your lips of tenderness
—Oh, I've loved you faithfully and well,
  Three years, or a bit less.
  It wasn't a success.

Thank God, that's done! and I'll take the road,
  Quit of my youth and you,
The Roman road to Wendover
  By Tring and Lilley Hoo,
  As a free man may do.

For youth goes over, the joys that fly
  The tears that follow fast;
And the dirtiest things we do must lie
  Forgotten at the last;
  Even Love goes past.

What's left behind I shall not find,
  The splendour and the pain;
The splash of sun, the shouting wind,
  And the brave sting of rain,
  I may not meet again.

But the years, that take the best away,
  Give something in the end;
And a better friend than love have they,
  For none to mar or mend,
  That have themselves to friend.

I shall desire and I shall find
  The best of my desires;
The autumn road, the mellow wind
  That soothes the darkening shires,
  And laughter, and inn-fires.

White mist about the black hedgerows,
  The slumbering Midland plain,
The silence where the clover grows,
  And the dead leaves in the lane,
  Certainly, these remain.

And I shall find some girl perhaps,
  And a better one than you,
With eyes as wise, but kindlier,
  And lips as soft, but true.
  And I daresay she will do.

1913

Home

I came back late and tired last night
    Into my little room,
To the long chair and the firelight
    And comfortable gloom.

But as I entered softly in
    I saw a woman there,
The line of neck and cheek and chin,
    The darkness of her hair,
The form of one I did not know
    Sitting in my chair.

I stood a moment fierce and still,
    Watching her neck and hair.
I made a step to her; and saw
    That there was no one there.

It was some trick of the firelight
    That made me see her there.
It was a chance of shade and light
    And the cushion in the chair.

Oh, all you happy over the earth,
    That night, how could I sleep?
I lay and watched the lonely gloom;
    And watched the moonlight creep
From wall to basin, round the room.
    All night I could not sleep.

1913

The Night Journey

Hands and lit faces eddy to a line;
   The dazed last minutes click; the clamour dies.
Beyond the great-swung arc o' the roof, divine,
   Night, smoky-scarv'd, with thousand coloured eyes

Glares the imperious mystery of the way.
   Thirsty for dark, you feel the long-limbed train
Throb, stretch, thrill motion, slide, pull out and sway,
   Strain for the far, pause, draw to strength again . . . .

As a man, caught by some great hour, will rise,
   Slow-limbed, to meet the light or find his love;
And, breathing long, with staring sightless eyes,
   Hands out, head back, agape and silent, move

Sure as a flood, smooth as a vast wind blowing;
   And, gathering power and purpose as he goes,
Unstumbling, unreluctant, strong, unknowing,
   Borne by a will not his, that lifts, that grows,

Sweep out to darkness, triumphing in his goal,
   Out of the fire, out of the little room . . . .
—There is an end appointed, O my soul!
   Crimson and green the signals burn; the gloom

Is hung with steam's far-blowing livid streamers.
   Lost into God, as lights in light, we fly,
Grown one with will, end-drunken huddled dreamers.
   The white lights roar. The sounds of the world die

And lips and laughter are forgotten things.
   Speed sharpens; grows. Into the night, and on,
The strength and splendour of our purpose swings.
   The lamps fade; and the stars. We are alone.

1913

The Way That Lovers Use

The way that lovers use is this;
   They bow, catch hands, with never a word,
And their lips meet, and they do kiss,
   —So I have heard.

They queerly find some healing so,
   And strange attainment in the touch;
There is a secret lovers know,
   —I have read as much.

And theirs no longer joy nor smart,
   Changing or ending, night or day;
But mouth to mouth, and heart on heart,
   —So lovers say.

   1913

Mutability

They say there's a high windless world and strange,
   Out of the wash of days and temporal tide,
   Where Faith and Good, Wisdom and Truth abide,
Æterna corpora, subject to no change.
There the sure suns of these pale shadows move;
   There stand the immortal ensigns of our war;
   Our melting flesh fixed Beauty there, a star,
And perishing hearts, imperishable Love . . . .

Dear, we know only that we sigh, kiss, smile;
   Each kiss lasts but the kissing; and grief goes over;
   Love has no habitation but the heart.
Poor straws! on the dark flood we catch awhile,
   Cling, and are borne into the night apart.
   The laugh dies with the lips, 'Love' with the lover.

SOUTH KENSINGTON – MAKAWELI, 1913

Clouds

Down the blue night the unending columns press
   In noiseless tumult, break and wave and flow,
   Now tread the far South, or lift rounds of snow
Up to the white moon's hidden loveliness.
Some pause in their grave wandering comradeless,
   And turn with profound gesture vague and slow,
   As who would pray good for the world, but know
Their benediction empty as they bless.

They say that the Dead die not, but remain
   Near to the rich heirs of their grief and mirth.
      I think they ride the calm mid-heaven, as these,
In wise majestic melancholy train,
      And watch the moon, and the still-raging seas,
   And men, coming and going on the earth.

THE PACIFIC, *October* 1913

Sonnet

(Suggested by some of the Proceedings of the Society for
Psychical Research)

Not with vain tears, when we're beyond the sun,
   We'll beat on the substantial doors, nor tread
   Those dusty high-roads of the aimless dead
Plaintive for Earth; but rather turn and run
Down some close-covered by-way of the air,
   Some low sweet alley between wind and wind,
   Stoop under faint gleams, thread the shadows, find
Some whispering ghost-forgotten nook, and there

Spend in pure converse our eternal day;
   Think each in each, immediately wise;
Learn all we lacked before; hear, know, and say
   What this tumultuous body now denies;
And feel, who have laid our groping hands away;
   And see, no longer blinded by our eyes.

1913

A Memory
(From a sonnet-sequence)

Somewhile before the dawn I rose, and stept
   Softly along the dim way to your room,
   And found you sleeping in the quiet gloom,
And holiness about you as you slept.
I knelt there; till your waking fingers crept
   About my head, and held it. I had rest
   Unhoped this side of Heaven, beneath your breast.
I knelt a long time, still; nor even wept.

It was great wrong you did me; and for gain
Of that poor moment's kindliness, and ease,
And sleepy mother-comfort!
                 Child, you know
How easily love leaps out to dreams like these,
Who has seen them true. And love that's wakened so
Takes all too long to lay asleep again.

WAIKIKI, *October* 1913

211

One Day

To-day I have been happy. All the day
   I held the memory of you, and wove
Its laughter with the dancing light o' the spray,
   And sowed the sky with tiny clouds of love,
And sent you following the white waves of sea,
   And crowned your head with fancies, nothing worth,
Stray buds from that old dust of misery,
   Being glad with a new foolish quiet mirth.

So lightly I played with those dark memories,
Just as a child, beneath the summer skies,
   Plays hour by hour with a strange shining stone,
For which (he knows not) towns were fire of old,
   And love has been betrayed, and murder done,
And great kings turned to a little bitter mould.

THE PACIFIC, *October* 1913

Waikiki

Warm perfumes like a breath from vine and tree
   Drift down the darkness. Plangent, hidden from eyes,
   Somewhere an *eukaleli* thrills and cries
And stabs with pain the night's brown savagery;
And dark scents whisper; and dim waves creep to me,
   Gleam like a woman's hair, stretch out, and rise;
   And new stars burn into the ancient skies,
Over the murmurous soft Hawaiian sea.

And I recall, lose, grasp, forget again,
   And still remember, a tale I have heard, or known,
An empty tale, of idleness and pain,
   Of two that loved—or did not love—and one
Whose perplexed heart did evil, foolishly,
A long while since, and by some other sea.

WAIKIKI, 1913

Hauntings

In the grey tumult of these after-years
   Oft silence falls; the incessant wranglers part;
And less-than-echoes of remembered tears
   Hush all the loud confusion of the heart;
And a shade, through the toss' d ranks of mirth and crying,
   Hungers, and pains, and each dull passionate mood,—
Quite lost, and all but all forgot, undying,
   Comes back the ecstasy of your quietude.

So a poor ghost, beside his misty streams,
Is haunted by strange doubts, evasive dreams,
   Hints of a pre-Lethean life, of men,
Stars, rocks, and flesh, things unintelligible,
   And light on waving grass, he knows not when,
And feet that ran, but where, he cannot tell.

THE PACIFIC, 1914

213

He Wonders Whether to Praise
or to Blame Her

I have peace to weigh your worth, now all is over,
  But if to praise or blame you, cannot say.
For, who decries the loved, decries the lover;
  Yet what man lauds the thing he's thrown away?

Be you, in truth, this dull, slight, cloudy naught,
  The more fool I, so great a fool to adore;
But if you're that high goddess once I thought,
  The more your godhead is, I lose the more.

Dear fool, pity the fool who thought you clever;
  Dear wisdom, do not mock the fool that missed you!
Most fair,—the blind has lost your face for ever!
  Most foul,—how could I see you while I kissed you?

So . . . the poor love of fools and blind I've proved you,
For, foul or lovely, 'twas a fool that loved you.

1913

Doubts

When she sleeps, her soul, I know,
Goes a wanderer on the air,
Wings where I may never go,
Leaves her lying, still and fair,
Waiting, empty, laid aside,
Like a dress upon a chair. . . .
This I know, and yet I know
Doubts that will not be denied.

For if the soul be not in place,
What has laid trouble in her face?
And, sits there nothing ware and wise
Behind the curtains of her eyes,
What is it, in the self's eclipse,
Shadows, soft and passingly,
About the corners of her lips,
The smile that is essential she?

And if the spirit be not there,
Why is fragrance in the hair?

1913

There's Wisdom in Women

'Oh love is fair, and love is rare;' my dear one she said,
　'But love goes lightly over.' I bowed her foolish head.
And kissed her hair and laughed at her. Such a child was she;
　So new to love, so true to love, and she spoke so bitterly.

But there's wisdom in women, of more than they have known,
　And thoughts go blowing through them, are wiser than their own,
Or how should my dear one, being ignorant and young,
　Have cried on love so bitterly, with so true a tongue?

June 1913

Fafaïa

Stars that seem so close and bright,
Watched by lovers through the night,
Swim in emptiness, men say,
Many a mile and year away.

And yonder star that burns so white,
May have died to dust and night
Ten, maybe, or fifteen year,
Before it shines upon my dear.

Oh! often among men below,
Heart cries out to heart, I know,
And one is dust a many years,
Child, before the other hears.

Heart from heart is all as far,
Fafaïa, as star from star.

SAANAPU, *November* 1913

216

Heaven

Fish (fly-replete, in depth of June,
Dawdling away their wat'ry noon)
Ponder deep wisdom, dark or clear,
Each secret fishy hope or fear.
Fish say, they have their Stream and Pond;
But is there anything Beyond?
This life cannot be All, they swear,
For how unpleasant, if it were!
One may not doubt that, somehow, Good
Shall come of Water and of Mud;
And, sure, the reverent eye must see
A Purpose in Liquidity.
We darkly know, by Faith we cry,
The future is not Wholly Dry.
Mud unto mud!—Death eddies near—
Not here the appointed End, not here!
But somewhere, beyond Space and Time,
Is wetter water, slimier slime!
And there (they trust) there swimmeth One
Who swam ere rivers were begun,
Immense, of fishy form and mind,
Squamous, omnipotent, and kind;
And under that Almighty Fin,
The littlest fish may enter in.
Oh! never fly conceals a hook,
Fish say, in the Eternal Brook,
But more than mundane weeds are there,
And mud, celestially fair;

Fat caterpillars drift around,
And Paradisal grubs are found;
Unfading moths, immortal flies,
And the worm that never dies.
And in that Heaven of all their wish,
There shall be no more land, say fish.

1913

The Great Lover

I have been so great a lover: filled my days
So proudly with the splendour of Love's praise,
The pain, the calm, and the astonishment,
Desire illimitable, and still content,
And all dear names men use, to cheat despair,
For the perplexed and viewless streams that bear
Our hearts at random down the dark of life.
Now, ere the unthinking silence on that strife
Steals down, I would cheat drowsy Death so far,
My night shall be remembered for a star
That outshone all the suns of all men's days.
Shall I not crown them with immortal praise
Whom I have loved, who have given me, dared with me
High secrets, and in darkness knelt to see
The inenarrable godhead of delight?
Love is a flame:—we have beaconed the world's night.
A city:—and we have built it, these and I.
An emperor:—we have taught the world to die.
So, for their sakes I loved, ere I go hence,
And the high cause of Love's magnificence,
And to keep loyalties young, I'll write those names
Golden for ever, eagles, crying flames,
And set them as a banner, that men may know,
To dare the generations, burn, and blow
Out on the wind of Time, shining and streaming . . . .

These I have loved:
White plates and cups, clean-gleaming,
Ringed with blue lines; and feathery, faery dust;
Wet roofs, beneath the lamp-light; the strong crusts
Of friendly bread; and many-tasting food;
Rainbows; and the blue bitter smoke of wood;
And radiant raindrops couching in cool flowers;
And flowers themselves, that sway through sunny hours,
Dreaming of moths that drink them under the moon;
Then, the cool kindliness of sheets, that soon
Smooth away trouble; and the rough male kiss
Of blankets; grainy wood; live hair that is
Shining and free; blue-massing clouds; the keen

Unpassioned beauty of a great machine;
The benison of hot water; furs to touch;
The good smell of old clothes; and others such—
The comfortable smell of friendly fingers,
Hair's fragrance, and the musty reek that lingers
About dead leaves and last year's ferns. . . .
                                    Dear names,
And thousand other throng to me! Royal flames;
Sweet water's dimpling laugh from tap or spring;
Holes in the ground; and voices that do sing;
Voices in laughter, too; and body's pain,
Soon turned to peace; and the deep-panting train;
Firm sands; the little dulling edge of foam
That browns and dwindles as the wave goes home;
And washen stones, gay for an hour; the cold
Graveness of iron; moist black earthen mould,

Sleep; and high places; footprints in the dew;
And oaks ; and brown horse-chestnuts, glossy-new;
And new-peeled sticks; and shining pools on grass;—
All these have been my loves. And these shall pass,
Whatever passes not, in the great hour,
Nor all my passion, all my prayers, have power
To hold them with me through the gate of Death.
They'll play deserter, turn with the traitor breath,
Break the high bond we made, and sell Love's trust
And sacramented covenant to the dust.
—Oh, never a doubt but, somewhere, I shall wake,
And give what's left of love again, and make
New friends, now strangers . . . .
                              But the best I've known
Stays here, and changes, breaks, grows old, is blown
About the winds of the world, and fades from brains
Of living men, and dies,
                       Nothing remains.
O dear my loves, O faithless, once again
This one last gift I give: that after men
Shall know, and later lovers, far-removed,
Praise you, 'All these were lovely'; say, 'He loved.'

MATAIEA, 1914

Retrospect

In your arms was still delight,
Quiet as a street at night;
And thoughts of you, I do remember,
Were green leaves in a darkened chamber,
Were dark clouds in a moonless sky.
Love, in you, went passing by,
Penetrative, remote, and rare,
Like a bird in the wide air,
And, as the bird, it left no trace
In the heaven of your face.
In your stupidity I found
The sweet hush after a sweet sound.
All about you was the light
That dims the greying end of night;
Desire was the unrisen sun,
Joy the day not yet begun,
With tree whispering to tree,
Without wind, quietly.
Wisdom slept within your hair,
And Long-Suffering was there,
And, in the flowing of your dress,
Undiscerning Tenderness.
And when you thought, it seemed to me,
Infinitely, and like a sea,
About the slight world you had known
Your vast unconsciousness was thrown . . . .
   O haven without wave or tide!
Silence, in which all songs have died!
Holy book, where hearts are still!
And home at length under the hill!
O mother-quiet, breasts of peace,
   Where love itself would faint and cease
O infinite deep I never knew,
I would come back, come back to you,
Find you, as a pool unstirred,
Kneel down by you, and never a word,

Lay my head, and nothing said,
In your hands, ungarlanded;
And a long watch you would keep;
And I should sleep, and I should sleep!

MATAIEA, *January* 1914

Tiare Tahiti

Mamua, when our laughter ends,
And hearts and bodies, brown as white,
Are dust about the doors of friends,
Or scent a-blowing down the night,
Then, oh! then, the wise agree,
Comes our immortality.
Mamua, there waits a land
Hard for us to understand.
Out of time, beyond the sun,
All are one in Paradise,
You and Pupure are one,
And Taü, and the ungainly wise.
There the Eternals are, and there
The Good, the Lovely, and the True,
And Types, whose earthly copies were
The foolish broken things we knew;
There is the Face, whose ghosts we are;
The real, the never-setting Star;
And the Flower, of which we love
Faint and fading shadows here;
Never a tear, but only Grief;
Dance, but not the limbs that move;
Songs in Song shall disappear;
Instead of lovers, Love shall be;
For hearts, Immutability;
And there, on the Ideal Reef,
Thunders the Everlasting Sea!
   And my laughter, and my pain,
Shall home to the Eternal Brain.
And all lovely things, they say,
Meet in Loveliness again;
Miri's laugh, Teïpo's feet,
And the hands of Matua,
Stars and sunlight there shall meet,
Coral's hues and rainbows there,
And Teüra's braided hair;
And with the starred *tiare's* white,
And white birds in the dark ravine,

And *flamboyants* ablaze at night,
And jewels, and evening's after-green,
And dawns of pearl and gold and red,
Mamua, your lovelier head!
And there'll no more be one who dreams
Under the ferns, of crumbling stuff,
Eyes of illusion, mouth that seems,
All time-entangled human love.
And you'll no longer swing and sway
Divinely down the scented shade,
Where feet to Ambulation fade,
And moons are lost in endless Day.
How shall we wind these wreaths of ours,
Where there are neither heads nor flowers?
Oh, Heaven's Heaven!—but we'll be missing
The palms, and sunlight, and the south;
And there's an end, I think, of kissing,
When our mouths are one with Mouth . . . .

   Taü here, Mamua,
Crown the hair, and come away!
Hear the calling of the moon,
And the whispering scents that stray
About the idle warm lagoon.
Hasten, hand in human hand,
Down the dark, the flowered way,
Along the whiteness of the sand,
And in the water's soft caress,
Wash the mind of foolishness,
Mamua, until the day.
Spend the glittering moonlight there
Pursuing down the soundless deep
Limbs that gleam and shadowy hair,
Or floating lazy, half-asleep.
Dive and double and follow after,
Snare in flowers, and kiss, and call,
With lips that fade, and human laughter
And faces individual,
Well this side of Paradise!. . .
There's little comfort in the wise.

   PAPEETE, *February* 1914

223

The Treasure

When colour goes home into the eyes,
    And lights that shine are shut again,
With dancing girls and sweet birds' cries
    Behind the gateways of the brain;
And that no-place which gave them birth, shall close
The rainbow and the rose:—

Still may Time hold some golden space
    Where I'll unpack that scented store
Of song and flower and sky and face,
    And count, and touch, and turn them o'er,
Musing upon them; as a mother, who
Has watched her children all the rich day through,
Sits, quiet-handed, in the fading light,
When children sleep, ere night.

August 1914

I. Peace

Now, God be thanked Who has matched us with His hour,
    And caught our youth, and wakened us from sleeping,
With hand made sure, clear eye, and sharpened power,
    To turn, as swimmers into cleanness leaping,
Glad from a world grown old and cold and weary,
    Leave the sick hearts that honour could not move,
And half-men, and their dirty songs and dreary,
    And all the little emptiness of love!

Oh! we, who have known shame, we have found release there,
    Where there's no ill, no grief, but sleep has mending.
        Naught broken save this body, lost but breath;
Nothing to shake the laughing heart's long peace there
    But only agony, and that has ending;
        And the worst friend and enemy is but Death.

II. Safety

Dear! of all happy in the hour, most blest
   He who has found our hid security,
Assured in the dark tides of the world that rest,
   And heard our word, 'Who is so safe as we ?'
We have found safety with all things undying,
   The winds, and morning, tears of men and mirth,
The deep night, and birds singing, and clouds flying,
   And sleep, and freedom, and the autumnal earth.
We have built a house that is not for Time's throwing.
   We have gained a peace unshaken by pain for ever.
War knows no power. Safe shall be my going,
   Secretly armed against all death's endeavour;
Safe though all safety's lost; safe where men fall;
And if these poor limbs die, safest of all.

III. The Dead

Blow out, you bugles, over the rich Dead!
   There's none of these so lonely and poor of old,
   But, dying, has made us rarer gifts than gold.
These laid the world away; poured out the red
Sweet wine of youth; gave up the years to be
   Of work and joy, and that unhoped serene,
   That men call age; and those who would have been,
Their sons, they gave, their immortality.

Blow, bugles, blow! They brought us, for our dearth,
   Holiness, lacked so long, and Love, and Pain.
Honour has come back, as a king, to earth,
   And paid his subjects with a royal wage;
And Nobleness walks in our ways again;
   And we have come into our heritage.

IV. The Dead

These hearts were woven of human joys and cares,
    Washed marvellously with sorrow, swift to mirth.
The years had given them kindness. Dawn was theirs,
    And sunset, and the colours of the earth.
These had seen movement, and heard music; known
    Slumber and waking; loved; gone proudly friended;
Felt the quick stir of wonder; sat alone;
    Touched flowers and furs and cheeks. All this is ended.

There are waters blown by changing winds to laughter
And lit by the rich skies, all day. And after,
    Frost, with a gesture, stays the waves that dance
And wandering loveliness. He leaves a white
    Unbroken glory, a gathered radiance,
A width, a shining peace, under the night.

V. The Soldier

If I should die, think only this of me:
    That there's some corner of a foreign field
That is for ever England. There shall be
    In that rich earth a richer dust concealed;
A dust whom England bore, shaped, made aware,
    Gave, once, her flowers to love, her ways to roam,
A body of England's, breathing English air,
    Washed by the rivers, blest by suns of home.

And think, this heart, all evil shed away,
    A pulse in the eternal mind, no less
        Gives somewhere back the thoughts by England
given;
Her sights and sounds; dreams happy as her day;
    And laughter, learnt of friends; and gentleness,
        In hearts at peace, under an English heaven.

226

Fragment

I strayed about the deck, an hour, to-night
Under a cloudy moonless sky; and peeped
In at the windows, watched my friends at table,
Or playing cards, or standing in the doorway,
Or coming out into the darkness. Still
No one could see me.

                I would have thought of them
—Heedless, within a week of battle—in pity,
Pride in their strength and in the weight and firmness
And link'd beauty of bodies, and pity that
This gay machine of splendour 'ld soon be broken,
Thought little of, pashed, scattered . . . .

                  Only, always,
I could but see them—against the lamplight—pass
Like coloured shadows, thinner than filmy glass,
Slight bubbles, fainter than the wave's faint light,
That broke to phosphorus out in the night,
Perishing things and strange ghosts—soon to die
To other ghosts—this one, or that, or I.

April 1915

The Dance
A Song

As the Wind, and as the Wind,
In a corner of the way,
Goes stepping, stands twirling,
Invisibly, comes whirling,
Bows before, and skips behind,
In a grave, an endless play—

So my Heart, and so my Heart,
Following where your feet have gone,
Stirs dust of old dreams there;
He turns a toe; he gleams there,
Treading you a dance apart.
But you see not, You pass on.

April 1915